Marriage Bonds
and
Ministers' Returns
of
Brunswick County
Virginia

- 1750-1810 -

I0091045

Compiled By:
Catherine Lindsay Knorr

Southern Historical Press, Inc.
Greenville, South Carolina

SOUTHERN HISTORICAL PRESS, INC.
PO BOX 1267
Greenville, SC   29601

ISBN #0-89308-261-9

Printed in the United States of America

TO

THE GRACIOUS COUNTY CLERKS

OF VIRGINIA

AND

THEIR CHARMING DEPUTIES

WHO, BY THEIR COURTESY, HELPFULNESS

AND ENCOURAGEMENT HAVE

MADE MY WORK A

NEVER ENDING PLEASURE.

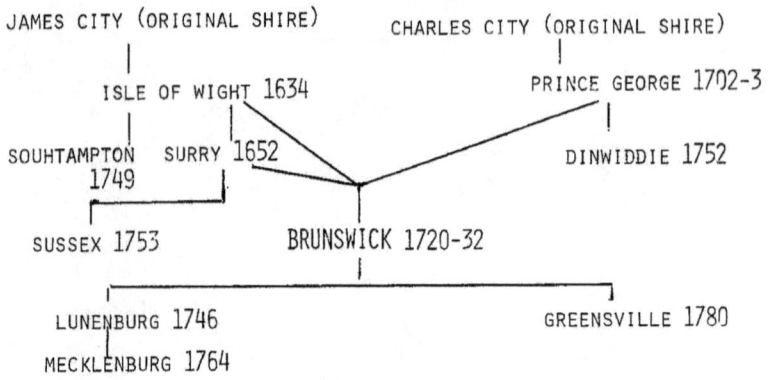

JAMES CITY (ORIGINAL SHIRE)   CHARLES CITY (ORIGINAL SHIRE)

ISLE OF WIGHT 1634   PRINCE GEORGE 1702-3

SOUHTAMPTON   SURRY 1652   DINWIDDIE 1752
    1749

SUSSEX 1753   BRUNSWICK 1720-32

LUNENBURG 1746   GREENSVILLE 1780

MECKLENBURG 1764

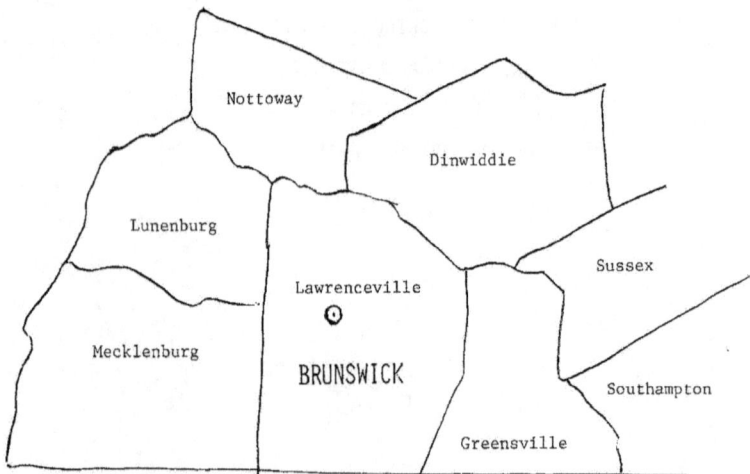

Nottoway

Dinwiddie

Lunenburg

Lawrenceville
⊙
Sussex

Mecklenburg   BRUNSWICK

Southampton

Greensville

iv

Publisher's Preface

Mrs. Knorr died in 1975, and after her death these books of
marriage records were kept in print and sold by her late husband.
Upon his death, they became the property of her grandson,
Hal Wyche Greer, III, of Marietta, Georgia, who continued to sell
them on a limited basis.

In mid-1981 I sought to find Mr. Greer to discuss with him
the possibility of obtaining the exclusive publishing and sales
rights to these 14 titles. In due time, Mr. Greer and I were
able to negotiate a contract for my exclusive sales and publica-
tion rights to these books. It was agreed that Mr. Greer would
have a final voice on the changing of the format of any of these
titles when they needed to be reprinted. I suggested to Mr. Greer
that when these various books sold out and a reprinting had to be
done, that for the sake of cost, I would publish them in a 6" x 9"
page size, but that the format and style would remain the same,
and this was agreed upon.

The reader is cautioned to note that these new 6 x 9 pages
are typed verbatum from Mrs. Knorr's original copy, and page by
page, so that new indexing was not required. It was also
decided that when a book went out of print, it would be retyped
on an electric typewriter with a carbon ribbon for better
legibility. As publisher, I felt it was important to call to
the attention of the reader these changes and the reason for
eventually bringing out all of these titles in a 6 x 9 book.

The Rev. S. Emmett Lucas, Jr.
Publisher

Preface

Did I say there was nothing in the world as peaceful as a Virginia court house? I take it all back. That was before I went to Brunswick.

There's nothing peaceful about Brunswick. There was so much going on I could hardly stay indoors and attend to my business.

But the only thing I really missed was the jail break. From my ground floor room at the inn I could look smack through the jail across the street. When the break took place it was after midnight and I was busy writing Easter cards to the folks back home.

I did see the fire sale. It was held in a tobacco warehouse (no use to say "huge": all tobacco warehouses are huge) across the side street. In my ignorance I though they had tobacco at the fire sale but it turned out to be merchandize from a department store. Nobody could use either street on account of the curb-to-curb crowd.

One night there was a dance in another tobacco warehouse. The music floated in to me as well as the happy sound of young people having fun until all hours. I loved all of it.

Then there was the stew. Sure 'nough stew, presided over by two white clad colored men stirring with what look to my cotton-patch eyes to be six foot lengths of 1x4 flooring which they used like canoe paddles. It was just before Easter and one of the churches was having a supper in - you guessed it - another tobacco warehouse. The cooking took place on the court house lawn, right under the Clerk's window, in a plack iron pot big enough to set up housekeeping in.

It was about the stew that I disgraced myself by asking if it were Mulligan stew only to be told with gentle courtesy, "No, Brunswick". I was as abashed as Kipling was when he poked the fire with Otheris' bayonet and Learoyd spoke to him.

I had fun in Brunswick, looking and listening and copying marriages on the side. The personnel of the court house as Lawrenceville is made up of as courteous, helpful and charming people as it has even been my happy privilege to be thrown with. There is the County Clerk, Mr. W. Emory Elmore, the Deputy Clerk, Mrs. Willie B. Abernathy and the Deputy's deputy (even mine, when it came to catching a bus 9 miles away!) her nephew, Julian Scarborough. Julian helps everybody.

Miss Willie engaged my room for me helped me when I needed it, even let me work one night so I could finish in the time I had allotted myself.

Brunswick is truly a delightful place. I thought as I worked of the charming names in the County from which early surveyors took their points and boundaries; Gum Grove, Luster Lane, Old Plank Road, Pigeon Roost Creek, Pea Hill Plantation, Quarrell Swamp, Indian Head Branch, and Rose's Creek.

Brunswick County was formed 1720 from Prince George, Surry and Isle of Wight being one of the three Virginia Counties named in honor of King George I of England whose title had been Duke of Brunswick (Long's Virginia County Names   p 48).

The first two pages of the Brunswick Order Book No. I are missing. On page 3 it is stated that a court was held for Brunswick the first day of July 1732, with the following gentlemen justices present: George Walton, Charles King, William Wynne and William Maclin. The first clerk was Drury Stith.

The first representation the new county had in the Assembly was the session of 5 August 1736 when Henry Embry and John Wall were Burgesses. (Stanard's Colonial Virginia Register p 108). The first marriage recorded was in 1750.

From Lawrenceville I went to Richmond to check the Brunswick bonds against the Richmond copy. The Brunswick list is alphabetically arranged and the Richmond list chronologically arranged. Since it took less time to copy the entire list than to check one against the other that is what I did.

In 1927 the Brunswick County officials employed some one to copy the loose marriage bonds. This was done, the marriages alphabetically arranged and copied in a book. Up to and including 1810 there are 1,470 marriages entered.

Then in 1938 the loose bonds were sent for safe keeping in fireproof quarters to the Virginia State Library, Archives Division, Richmond. Here, in 1941, they were copied again by Miss Stella Bass of the Virginia State Library Staff. These are arranged chronologically in a large Marriage Register. There are 1,501 entries up to and including 1810-31 more than the Brunswick copy.

These data do not always aree with the Brunswick list. Where there is a discrepancy in the groom's name I have made two cards. In the case of a discrepancy in the bride's name it has been noted on the card - "Bowler Dobbins married Jane Hearn": "Brunswick says Ann Hearn". All discrepancies have been checked by the original bonds not just one list against the other. For instance: Virginia State Library list says Mark Green married Patsey Warwick. The Brunswick copy says Mark Green married Patsy Harwell. Her own consent is with the original bond signed Patsey Warwick, dated 14 December 1797. So the Brunswick copy is clearly wrong. Again: The Virginia State Library copy was Partain Bass married Rebecca Tatum 4 January 1786. The Ministers' Returns say Partain Bass and Rebecca Tatum were married in St. Andrew's Parish by the Rev. Thomas Lundie, Rector of St. Andrew's Parish. Now the Brunswick list says Bertram Bass married Rebecca Tatum 4 January 1786. It would seem that two against one, the name is surely Partain and not Bertram. Then we have further proof in the marriage of

Hardiman Ivey and Elizabeth Bass 23 July 1806: Partain and Rebecca Bass consent. Batts Tatum is witness. Again the Brunswick list is clearly wrong.

The reference paging given in this book is from the Virginia State Library copy except where it states "Brunswick p.33". There are several reasons for this. For the same period 1750-1810 there are 31 more marriages in the Virginia State Library copy than in the Brunswick copy, also, the Vriginia State Library gives middle names and the Brunswick copy initials only. Then if any one cares to check the information contained in this book he or she would have to revert to the original bonds which are in the Archives department of the Virginia State Library.

The Ministers' Returns starting 1782 and in the back of the Virginia State Library copy of Brunswick Marriages. They do not appear in the Brunswick copy. They are very important. Copied and checked against the bonds, it will be seen there are many marriages in the Ministers' Returns for which there are no bonds. This book contains 208 of them between 1782-1810.

In July 1898 there was published a list of Brunswick county marriage bonds in the William and Mary Quarterly, Vol. VII pp 37-38: again a much larger Brunswick list was published in 1911 in the same magazine Vol. XX pp 195-210 inclusive. In April 1920 the Virginia magazine published a list of Brunswick marriages, continued in October 1921, Vol. XXIX pp 166-168 inclusive, and 508-510 inclusive.

All three of these lists have been carefully checked against both the Brunswick and the Virginia State Library lists. Result: an even dozen marriages that did not appear in the other two lists. They are included with their exact references. These three lists were published before the Brunswick list was made and it is highly probable that there were loose bonds then that had disappeared by 1927.

Brunswick had its share of confused spelling: Cheley - Cheely; Hix - Hicks; Canady - Kennedy; Wray - Ray; House - Howse - Howze; Dugger - Duggar; Sanders - Saunders; Rhese - Rese - Reese; Mathis - Mathews - Matthews.

This volume, with 1,778 entries, is the largest to date in my series of Virginia County Marriages. And it has been the most work because I had so many sources to copy and check. But it has been fun, too, and I hope you like it.

Mrs. H. A. Knorr
1401 Linden Street
Pine Bluff, Arkansas

MARRIAGES OF
BRUNSWICK COUNTY, VIRGINIA
1750 - 1810

14 October 1786. Charles ABERNATHY and Elizabeth Davenport. Sur. Harberd
Abernathy. Wit. Joshua Abernathy. p 41

22 November 1802. Charles ABERNATHY and Nancy W. Croft. This is an
error. It is Miles Abernathy in the original bond. See Miles
Abernathy. Brunswick p 22

7 April 1809. Elisha ABERNATHY and Nancy Read, dau. Susanna Reas. Sur.
Robert Lucy. p 171

11 February 1795. Frederick ABERNATHY and Milly Davenport, 21, and a
resident of the County 6 months. Sur. Alexander Andrews. Wit. Allen
Abernathy. Married 13 February by the Rev. Peter Wynne. p 84

9 August 1804. George ABERNATHY and Polly Tucker. Married by the Rev.
Peter Wynne. Ministers' Returns p 382

22 August 1788. Harbert ABERNATHY and Susanna Harwell. Sur. Samuel
Harwell, Sr. p 52

10 December 1796. Henry ABERNATHY and Rebecca Firth, dau. Sarah Firth.
Sur. Rowley Brown. Wit. Davis Brown and Thomas Firth. Married 15 Dec.
by the Rev. Aaron Brown, Methodist. p 93

22 March 1802. James ABERNATHY and Frances M. Ginnings or Jennings, dau.
Rebecca Ginnings. Sur. Hubbard Saunders. Wit. Jeremiah Miskell,
Chloe Saunders and Mary Ann Turbyfill. Married by the Rev. Hubbard
Saunders who say Jennings. p 133

7 January 1794. Jarrard ABERNATHY and Anney Sadler, dau. Featherstone
Sadler. Sur. Edward F. Sadler. Wit. Thomas Sadler. Married
9 January by the Rev. Aaron Brown, Methodist. p 79

17 August 1803. John ABERNATHY and Elizabeth Sturdivant. Married by the
Rev. Peter Wynne. Ministers' Returns p 381

1 February 1809. John ABERNATHY, Jr. and Nancy Kelly. Sur. James Kelly.
Married 4 February by the Rev. Peter Wynne. p 170

3 April 1806. John ABERNATHY and Blanche Elder. Married by the Rev.
Peter Wynne. Ministers' Returns p 382

22 November 1802. Miles ABERNATHY and Nancy W. Croft. Sur. Washington
Croft. Married 9 December by the Rev. Aaron Brown, Methodist, who
says Miles. p 137

- July 1785. James ADAMS and Mary Adams. Married by the Rev. Thomas
Lundie, Rector of St. Andrews' Parish. Ministers' Returns p 345

10 October 1801. Thomas ADAMS and Lucy Orgain. Sur. Herbert Hill.
Married 15 October by the Rev. Aaron Brown, Methodist. p 128

1

22 October 1804. William ADAMS and Lucy Harper. Married by the Rev. Peter Wynne. Ministers' Returns p 380

26 September 1796. Zadock ADAMS and Elizabeth Parish, 21. Sur. William Parish. Wit. James Parish. Married 8 October by the Rev. Aaron Brown, Methodist. p 91

27 July 1792. David ADDAMS and Darcus Bass, 21. (Adams) Benjamin Bass makes affidavit as to her age. Sur. Claiborne Cain. p 71

6 October 1810. Thomas ADKINS and Creecy Birdsong, dau. Merrit Birdsong. See Thomas Atkins. Brunswick p 22

2 April 1810. John ALEXANDER and Sally Thrower, dau. Edward Thrower. Sur. Henry Robinson. Married 5 April by the Rev. Cary James, Methodist. p 175

- January 1786. William ALEXANDER and Rebecca Hardaway Hatch of Bath Parish. Married by the Rev. Thomas Lundie, Rector of St. Andrews' Parish. Ministers' Returns p 347

9 November 1802. William ALEXANDER and Elizabeth Lane, dau. Sylvia Harris. Sur. Edmund Lane. Married 10 November by the Rev. Aaron Brown, Methodist. p 136

28 November 1785. Howell ALLEN and Mary Edwards. Sur. Harbert Edwards. p 36

27 August 1792. Howell ALLEN and Rebecca Williams, 21. Sur. Isaac Williams. Married 12 September by the Rev. Edward Dromgoole. p 71

28 July 1806. Reuben ALLEN and Elizabeth Lucy, over 21. Sur. William Sturdivant. Wit. Thomas Stith. Married 21 August by the Rev. Peter Wynne. p 157

27 December 1792. William ALLEN, Jr. and Lucy Brewer, dau. William Brewer. Sur. Morris Pearson. Returned 10 January 1793 by the Rev. Edward Dromgoole. p 73

7 December 1805. William ALLEN and Sally W. Tarpley, 21. Sur. Jeremiah W. Hampton. Wit. Robert Kennedy and Jesse Kennedy. Married 10 December by the Rev. Peter Wynne. p 153

19 December 1805. Wyatt ALLEN and Nancy Tarver, dau. Andrew Tarver. Sur. Wilson Williams. p 153

18 September 1803. Richard ALLEY and Polley Alley, 21. Drury Alley, father (which?) Sur. William Linch. Richard Alley under age. Married 19 September by the Rev. Edward Dromgoole. p 142

15 January 1809. Edward ALLMAND and Mary Easter, widow. Sur. William Pritchett. p 170

5 March 1810. Caleb ANDERSON and Frances L. James, dau. John P. James.
Sur. Robert L. James. Wit. Abner Wesson and John Braswell. Married
by the Rev. Cary James, Methodist. p 174

7 April 1779. Churchill ANDERSON and Rebecca Hall, dau. Patrick Hall.
Sur. Thomas Camp. Wit. Salley Camp. p 22

24 July 1753. Claiborne ANDERSON and Elizabeth Clack. Sur. James Clack.
Wit. B. Watkins and W. Battersby. Claiborne Anderson from Chester-
field County and ward of Richard Eppes who consents. p 1

29 December 1810. Nathan ANDERSON and Elizabeth Pritchett. Sur. James
Trotter. p 178

22 November 1784. John ANDERTON and Clarissa Durham. Sur. Mordecai
Howard. p 34

3 November 1796. William ANDERTON and Macarina Ragland. Sur. Freeman
Penticost. Wit. William Andrews, Jr. p 92

8 January 1798. Alexander ANDREWS and Martha Moore, 21, lived in County
6 months. Sur. Thomas Moore. Wit. Thomas Moore, Jr. and Mary
Thomson. Married 9 January by the Rev. Aaron Brown, Methodist. p 103.

29 October 1787. David ANDREWS and Elizabeth King. Sur. Howell Dugger.
Wit. Thomas Moore and Henry King. David Andrews son of John Andrews.
p 47

28 May 1787. John ANDREWS and Mary Edwards. Sur. John Edwards.
Married by the Rev. Thomas Lundie, Rector of St. Andrew's Parish.
p. 45

14 December 1805. Wilkins ANDRUS and Susanna Pegram. Married by the
Rev. Peter Wynne. Ministers' Returns p 382

12 January 1788. Thomas APELIN and Susanna McKenny. This is an error;
the name is Asselin in original bond. See Thomas Asselin.
Brunswick p 24

21 December 1790. Amos ARCHER and Fanny Harrison. Sur. William Harrison.
Wit. C. R. Jones, George Jones and John Harrison. Dau. Thomas
Harrison. Married by the Rev. John King, Baptist. p 62

26 October 1808. John ARCHER and Jean Barrow. Sur. Dennis Barrow. p 168

26 December 1786. Richard ARRINGTON and Catharine Carter, under age.
George Malone gives consent. Sur. Arthur Freeman. Richard Arring-
ton of Halifax Co. Married by the Rev. Thomas Lundie, Rector of
St. Andrew's Parish. p 42

12 January 1788. Thomas Asselin and Susanna McKenny, dau. John McKenny
who is surety. Married by the Rev. Thomas Lundie, Rector. of St.
Andrew's Parish who say Asselin. p 49

25 November 1794. George ATKINS and Mary Simms, 21. Sur Phil Claiborne.
Wit. John Claiborne. Married by the Rev. Edward Dromgoole. p 83

3 September 1802. George ATKINS and Lucretia Taylor. Sur. John Wyche. Wit. He. (?) Parham. Married 16 September by the Rev. Ira Ellis. p 135

6 October 1810. Thomas ATKINS and Creacy Birdsong, dau. Merrit Birdsong. Sur. Gabriel Harrison. Wit. David Cooks and Rebecca Birdsong. See Thomas Adkins. p 176

8 December 1806. William ATKINS and Sarah Burge. Sur. William Rice. Married 11 December by the Rev. Peter Wynne. p 159

25 August 1800. John ATKINSON and Elizabeth Lundie, 21. Sur. Charles Cheely. Wit. Susanna Bolling and Lucy Lundie. Married 5 September by the Rev. Hubbard Saunders. p 122

27 December 1790. Thomas ATKINSON and Elizabeth Collier. See Thomas Atkison. Brunswick p 26

26 August 1782. William ATKINSON and Mary Hix. Sur. Edward Tatum. p 29

22 June 1789. William ATKINSON and Sarah Parham. Sur. James Parham. Wit. Absaleme Atkinson and Jesse Atkinson. Married by the Rev. Thomas Lundie, Rector of St. Andrew's Parish. p 55

27 December 1790. Thomas ATKINSON and Elizabeth Collier, dau. Charles Collier. Sur. William Atkinson. Wit. William Smith Collier. Married by the Rev. John King, Baptist. See Thomas Atkinson. p 62

22 June 1774. Peter AVENT and Elizabeth Sims. Sur. John Avent. p 15

17 March 1800. Barrington AVERY and Rebecca Mitchell. Sur. Peter Hawthorne. Wit. Kennon H. Dixon. Married 20 March by the Rev. Peter Wynne. p 120

26 September 1808. Tilman AVERY and Temperance Edwards. Sur. John Wynne. p 168

19 May 1808. William AVERY and Clary Hunt. Married by the Rev. Peter Wynne. Ministers' Returns p 389

24 June 1794. Henry BAILEY and Sarah Jackson. Sur. Henry Jackson. p 81

31 March 1794. John BAILEY and Jane Mitchell. Sur. William Mitchell. Married 3 April by the Rev. Aaron Brown, Methodist. p 80

28 January 1797. John BAILEY and Amey Danman. Sur. Simon Laffoon. Brunswick say Dunman. Married 31 January by the Rev. Aaron Brown, Methodist. p 96

22 October 1802. Thomas S. BAILEY and Hannah Jackson. Sur. Robert Jackson. Married 23 October by the Rev. Aaron Brown, Methodist. p 136

13 February 1809. John BAIRD and Jean Reade, 21. Sur. John Mosby. Married 15 February by the Rev. Edward Dromgoole. p 170

26 March 1770. John BAKER and Patty Harris, dau. Henry Harris of Southhampton County. Sur. Henry Mounger. Wit. John Harris and West Harris. p 8

27 December 1802. Charles BALENTINE (Ballentine?) and Betsy Brown. Sur. Peter Read. Married 29 December by the Rev. Ira Ellis. p 138

22 September 1807. William BANKS and Polly G. Jinkins. Sur. John Wyche. Married 24 September by the Rev. Aaron Brown, Methodist. p 163

13 February 1806. Drury J. BARNER and Sally Taylor, dau. Luke and Elizabeth Taylor. Sur. Green Hall. p 155

July 1787 - July 1788. Francis BARNER and Elizabeth Mays. Married by the Rev. Thomas Lundie, Rector of St. Andrew's Parish. Ministers' Returns p 351

20 March 1788. James BARNES and Sally Browder, born 17 March 1767, dau. Joseph and Suky Browder. Sur. William Connelly and Thomas Lundie. Married by the Rev. Thomas Lundie, Rector of St. Andrew's Parish. p 50

6 January 1802. James BARNES and Nancy Hammon, dau. William Hammon. Sur. Joseph Rash. p 132

23 December 1786. Stephen BARNES and Sarah Johnson, of age, dau. William and Rachel Johnson. Sur. Allen Johnson. Stephen Barnes ward of John Powell. Married by the Rev. Thomas Lundie, Rector of St. Andrew's Parish. p 42

22 June 1793. John BARNETT, Jr., and Nancy Nipper, dau. James Nipper. Sur. John Harrison. Wit. Thomas Griffeth, Thomas Washington, and Dennis Dayley. John Barnett, Jr., son of John Barnett, Sr. p 76.

26 October 1808. Dennis BARROW and Ermine Daniel. Sur. John Archer. Married 2 November by the Rev. Peter Wynne. p 168

13 August 1803. John BARROW and Jincey Johnson, dau. John Johnson. Sur. Benjamin Johnson. Wit. Thomas Harvey. Married 16 August by the Rev. Aaron Brown, Methodist, who says Jean. p 141

4 January 1786. Bertram BASS and Rebecca Tatum. This is an error. The name is Partain Bass. See Partain Bass. Brunswick p 30

23 April 1803. Edmund BASS and Eliza H. Ingram. Sur. John Ingram. p 140

25 February 1799. Ephraim BASS and Patsey Lanier. Sur. John Lanier. Married 14 March by the Rev. Aaron Brown, Methodist. p 111

22 February 1797. Frederick BASS and Polly Vaughan, dau. James Vaughan. Sur. Herbert Hill. Wit. Robert Vaughan. Brunswick says Frederick Bass, Jr. p 97

27 September 1802. Hartwell BASS and Frances Mason. Sur. David Jackson.
Married 14 October by the Rev. Edward Dromgoole. p 135

23 December 1778. Henry BASS and Elizabeth Rivers, dau. William Rivers.
Sur. Robert Slate. p 21

23 January 1810. James BASS and Polly Green. Married by the Rev. Peter
Wynne. Ministers' Returns p 392

24 October 1791. John BASS and Nancy Saunders. Sur. Thomas Saunders.
Married 1 November by the Rev. Aaron Brown, Methodist. p 66

24 October 1791. John H. BASS and Rebecca Pittello. Sur. James
Pittello. p 66

28 January 1805. Nathan BASS and Martha Beatey or Betty. Sur. David
Kirkland. Wit. John H. Bass. Married 31 January by the Rev.
Hubbard Saunders. p 150

4 January 1786. Partain BASS and Rebecca Tatum, dau. Joseph Tatum,
deceased. Sur. John Parrish. Wit. John Hicks Bass. Both of St.
Andrew's Parish. Married by the Rev. Thomas Lundie, Rector. p 38

14 October 1800. Thomas BASS and Sarah Adams, 35. Sur. Partin Bass.
Wit. John Greene. p 123

28 March 1808. Thomas BASS and Sally Fletcher. Sur. Elisha Clarke.
Married 14 April by the Rev. Edward Dromgoole. p 166

1 October 1805. Joel BAUGH and Elizabeth Hagood. Sur. Randolph Hagood.
Married 4 October by the Rev. Hubbard Saunders. p 152

17 June 1801. Littleberry BAUGH and Frances Wilkes, 21. Sur. Thomas
Wilkes. Married 18 June by the Rev. Hubbard Saunders. p 127.

5 September 1790. Barnet BEASLEY and Susannah Baugh, dau. Daniel Baugh
who is surety. Married 29 September by the Rev. John Easter. p 60

19 April 1809. Dr. Peter J. BEASLEY and Rebecca J. Fletcher. Consent
of N. Fletcher. Sur. Elisha Clark. Wit. J. B. Lockhart. Married
20 April by the Rev. Edward Dromgoole. p 171

28 June 1802. David BECK and Polley Hood. Sur. Peter Read. p 134

11 May 1808. Benjamin Bennett and Susan Taylor. Sur. William Taylor.
Married by the Rev. Thomas Adams, Methodist. p 166

27 April 1801. Maclin BENNETT and Judith Bennett, 21. Sur. David
Dugger. Wit. John Dugger, Jr. Returned 30 May by the Rev. Hubbard
Saunders. p 127

1 January 1782. Richard BENNETT and Mary Crook, dau. James Crook. Sur.
William Abernathy. Richard not 21, son of Benjamin Bennett. p 28

5 November 1787. William BENNETT and Mary Edwards. Sur. Daniel Dugger. Wit. Jesse Edwards and Burwell Edwards. Married by the Rev. Thomas Lundie, Rector of St. Andrew's Parish. p 47

28 April 1787. John BERRY and Anne Ingram, dau. Bartholomew Ingram. Sur. Joseph Lyell. Married by the Rev. Thomas Lundie, Rector of St. Andrew's Parish. p 44

21 December 1801. John J. BERRY and Mary W. Meredith, consent of David Meredith. Consent only. p 131

1 August 1793. William BERRY and Lucy Matthews, dau. Lucy Matthews. Sur. John Hampton. Wit. Mitty Smith and Edward Holmes. Married 5 August by the Rev. Daniel Southall. p 76

9 July 1800. William BERRY and Martha Collier, dau. Mary Collier. Sur. Nathaniel Collier. Wit. George Berry. Married by the Rev. Aaron Brown, Methodist. p 121

22 August 1809. Thomas BERTON and Patsey Jarrett. See Thomas Burton. Brunswick p 32

24 November 1795. Jesse BESHEARS and Betsey Shell, 21. Sur. William Shell. Wit. Thomas Moore and Lucy Shell. p 88

27 November 1786. Thomas BETHSHERS and Elizabeth Upchurch. Sur. Peter Read. Married by the Rev. John King, Baptist. p 42

27 November 1787. Thomas BETHSHURS and Elizabeth Whitechurch. This is an error. The original bond says Elizabeth Upchurch. Brunswick p 32

25 July 1801. John BETTY and Lucy Pettway. Sur. John Drummond, Jr. Married 30 July by the Rev. Balaam Ezell, Baptist. p 127

9 May 1797. Thomas BETTY and Martha Preston, 21. Sur. James Preston. Wit. Thomas Preston. p 98

31 December 1804. Thomas BETTY and Rebecca Finch. Sur. David Walter. p 149

24 December 1787. William BETTY and Mary Betty, dau. Thomas Betty. Sur. Edward Thrower. Married 5 January 1788 by the Rev. John King, Baptist. p 48

22 January 1798. William BETTY and Anne Bass. Sur. Herbert Hill. p 103

7 April 1783. Joel BIGGS and Nancy Elder, dau. Joseph Elder. p 30

12 December 1781. James BILBO and Dorotha Clack. Sur. William Thornton. James Bilbo of Mecklenburg County. p 27

7 September 1784. Nicholas BILBO and Mary Baskervill. Sur. George Hunt Baskervill. p 33

11 November 1806. Elias BILLINGSBY and Lucy Powell, 21. Sur. John
    Powell. p 158

5 September 1801. Augustus BILLOPS and Sinah Vaughan. Sur. William V.
    Avery. Married 8 September by the Rev. Hubbard Saunders who says
    Augustine. p 128

11 August 1797. Edward BIRCHETT and Polly Jackson, ward of Benjamin
    Lewis. Sur. John Orgain. Wit. John Watson. p 99

4 September 1793. Theodrick BIRCHETT and Rebecca Collier, dau. Howell
    Collier. See Theodrick BIRKETT. Brunswick p 34

23 March 1795. Battis BIRD and Susanna Lawrence, 21. William Abernathy
    and Thomas Ingram make affidavit as to her age. Sur. Thomas Ingram.
    Wit. Zachariah Lawrence, Miles Lawrence, Thomas Adkins, and
    William Berry. p 85

July 1789 - July 1790. Freeman BIRDSONG and Frances F -. Married by the
    Rev. Thomas Lundie, Rector of St. Andrew's Parish. Ministers'
    Returns p 356

20 April 1789. William BIRDSONG and Judith Cealey, dau. William Celey.
    Sur. Merrill Cealey. p 54

10 January 1807. William M. BIRDSONG and Rebecca H. Bass. Sur. Henry
    Birdsong. p 160

4 September 1793. Theodrick BIRKETT and Rebecca Collier, 21, dau. Howell
    Collier, deceased. Sur. Isaac Hicks. Wit. Bottom Steagall and Asa
    Gresham Sack. Pennington makes affidavit as to her age. See
    Theodrick Birchett. p 77

10 January 1793. John BISHOP and Elizabeth Jones, dau. John Jones.
    Sur. Charles Hill. John Bishop son of Mathnay Bishop. p 74

31 May 1793. Joseph Mason BISHOP and Marticia Wynne, dau. Thomas Wynne.
    Sur. William Bishop. Married 6 June by the Rev. John Neblett. p 75

30 March 1792. Robert BLACKWELL and Jinsey Jones, dau. Stephen Jones.
    Sur. John Jones, Jr. Wit. John Blackwell and Robert Jones.
    Married by the Rev. John Jones, Methodist. p 70

27 August 1810. Austin BLALOCK and Mansfield Mosley. Sur. Sion Linch.
    Married 8 September by the Rev. Cary James, Methodist, who says
    Augustine. p 176

22 May 1786. David BLALOCK and Karen Vaughan. Sur. James Vaughan.
    Brunswick says Kareh. p 39

26 December 1796. Richard BLALOCK and Tabitha Mize. Sur. Jeremiah
    Mize, Jr. Married 29 December by the Rev. Edward Dromgoole. p 95

17 December 1801. Ezekiel BLANCH and Milly Cook, of age, dau. Lucy Cook. Sur. Anselm Minor. Wit. Martha Cook and John Cook. p 130

23 February 1778. Ingram BLANKS and Patty Grigg, dau. Lewis Grigg. Sur. Matthew Davis. Wit. Jesse Grigg. p 19

9 October 1753. Richard BLANKS and Winifred House, widow. Sur. Andrew Troughton. Wit. Thomas Stith. p 1

28 November 1785. James BLICK and Sarah Baugh, dau. James Baugh, deceased and Sarah Baugh. Sur. Robert Rivers. Wit. Tabitha Baugh and Ben Blick. Both of St. Andrew's Parish. Married by the Rev. Thomas Lundie. p 36

27 August 1787. James BLICK and Catharine Lanier. Sur. William Lanier. Marriage by the Rev. Thomas Lundie, Rector of St. Andrew's Parish. p 45

14 October 1788. William BLUNT and Ann Gilliam, dau. John Gilliam. Sur. Hinchia Gilliam. Married by the Rev. Thomas Lundie, Rector of St. Andrew's Parish. p 51

4 October 1790. Robert BOLLING and Katharine Stith, consent of Buckner Stith, Sr. Sur. Griffin Stith. Wit. Buckner Stith, Jr. Robert Bolling of Petersburg, Dinwiddie County. Married by the Rev. Thomas Lundie, Rector of St. Andrew's Parish, who says Catharine. p 61

8 September 1807. Samuel BOLLING and Nancy Willis Elliott, dau. John Elliott. Sur. Phillip Pryor. p 163

29 October 1810. Benjamin BOOTH and Sally Hicks, dau. Isaac Hicks. Sur. George H. Jones. p 177

25 August 1802. Gilliam BOOTH and Rebecca Hicks. Sur. Isaac Hicks. Married 26 August by the Rev. Aaron Brown, Methodist. p 135

21 July 1797. Thomas BOOTH and Martha Harrison, 21. Sur. James H. Harrison. Wit. George H. Jones. p 99

28 September 1809. Robert C. BOOTH and Elizabeth B. Hicks, dau. Isaac Hicks. Sur. Stephen Jackson. p 172

3 January 1792. William BOSWELL and Mary Wall, dau. George Wall, deceased. Sur. Henry Robinson. Wit. Thomas Claiborne. Married 7 January by the Rev. Aaron Brown, Methodist. p 69

29 August 1800. William BOSWELL and Susan Lane. Sur. Herbert Hill. Wit. Edward Lane. Married 30 August by the Rev. Aaron Brown, Methodist. p 122

2 January 1810. Edward Branch BOTT and Sally Prudence Parham, dau. William Parham. Sur. William Longbottom. p 174

17 July 1800. John BOTTOM and Tabitha Harrison, 21. Sur. Henry Harrison. Wit. Weatherinton Preston. Married by the Rev. James Meacham. p 122

13 August 1798. Leonard BOWEN and Priscilla Paup. Sur. Henry Watson.
Wit. Nathaniel Collier. p 106

22 December 1792. Isaac Thompson BOWLES and Milly Huff, dau. Daniel
Huff. Sur. William Huff. p 73

13 December 1800. Isaac BOWLES and Timna Holloway, 21. Sur. Harrison
Barner. Wit. John Barner. p 124

23 January 1797. John BOWLES and Elizabeth Gilliam Barker, 21, dau.
Burrell Barker. Sur. Rodford Gunn. Wit. Balaam Ezell and George
Gunn. Married 31 January by the Rev. Balaam Ezell, Baptist. p 96

15 December 1802. Edward BOZEMAN and Susanna Quarles, 21. Sur. Creed
Quarles. Married 18 December by the Rev. Peter Wynne. p 137

22 September 1803. Thomas BOZEMAN and Rebecca Aldridge, 21. Sur. Creed
Quarles. p 142

1 April 1785. Samuel BRACEY and Tabitha Hicks, under age, dau. Robert
Hicks. Sur. Hamlin Hicks and Thomas N. Smith. Married by the Rev.
Edward Dromgoole. p 85

24 June 1794. Edward BRANCH and Sally Goodrich, 21, dau. Mary Goodrich.
Sur. Henry Bailey. Wit. John Goodrich and Lucy Sims. Married
26 June by the Rev. Edward Dromgoole. p 81

15 February 1797. Edward BRANCH and Martha Tilman, 21. Lucy Harrison
makes affidavit as to her age. Sur. Hartwell Bass. Wit. Frances
Green, Betsey Tillman and Polly Vaughan. Married 17 February by
the Rev. Edward Dromgoole. p 97

29 April 1794. James BRANN and Nancy Porter, dau. John Porter. Sur.
Joshua Porter. Wit. John Brann. p 81

12 January 1791. James BRANTLEY and Rebecca Stainback. Edward Robinson
and Lucy Stainback guardians of Rebecca. Sur. John Owen. Wit.
Robinson Stainback. Married by the Rev. John King, Baptist. p 63

7 July 1802. Jesse BRASINGTON and Martha Glandish. See Joseph
Brasington. Brunswick p 38

7 July 1802. Joseph BRASINGTON and Martha Glandish, of age. Sur.
Benjamin Glandish. Wit. Charles Harrison. Married 9 July by the
Rev. Hubbard Saunders who says Joseph. See Jesse Brasington. p 134

3 September 1810. Jesse BRASWELL and Winifred Nanny, of age. Sur. John
Smith. Married by the Rev. Cary James, Methodist. p 176

23 December 1799. John BRASWELL and Elizabeth James, 21. Sur. Absalom
Williams. Wit. Isaac Ledbetter. Married 25 December by the Rev.
Ballam Ezell, Baptist. p 117

21 November 1777. Vincent BRENT and Margaret Brent, dau. William Brent. Sur. Robert Spencer. p 18

27 December 1785. Bartlett BREWER and Biddy Cannon, widow. Sur. Newit Brewer. Of St. Andrew's Parish. Married by the Rev. Thomas Lundie who says Kennon. p 37

26 November 1787. John BREWER and Mary Mitchell, dau. Lockhart Mitchell. Sur. Braxton Robinson. p 47

18 December 1805. Kinchen BREWER and Patsey Pearson, 21. Sur. Johnson Pearson. p 153

27 August 1792. Newit BREWER and Elizabeth Purkinson. Sur. Isham Purkinson. p 71

27 August 1792. Newit BREWER and Elizabeth Nicholson. This is an error. The original bond says Elizabeth Purkinson. Brunswick p 38

10 December 1804. Thomas BRIDGE and Martha Bass. See Thomas Burge. Brunswick p 38

20 January 1792. John BRIDGEFORTH and Mary Miller, dau. Jacob Miller. Sur. Thomas Manson. Wit. Jacob Miller. Married by the Rev. Thomas Lundie, Rector of St. Andrew's Parish. p 69

11 June 1759. Thomas BRIDGES and Dorothy Vines, under 21. Sur. Thomas Vines. Wit. William Cryer. p 6

24 February 1772. Frederick BRIGGS and Molly Goodrich, consent of Edward Goodrich, Sr. Sur. Francis Young. Wit. James Young. p 11

31 December 1794. Allen BRINTLE and Susanna Reese, 21. Sur. Rawleigh Harvey. Wit. William Parish and Isham Reese. Married 1 January 1795 by the Rev. Peter Wynne. p 84

10 November 1797. Isaac BRITT and Molly Monk Huff. Sur. James Huff. Married 16 November by the Rev. Balaam Ezell, Baptist. p 100

23 July 1781. John BROADNAX and Martha Rivers, dau. Thomas Rivers. Sur. Hincha Mabry. Wit. Thomas Broadnax and Wilson Miles Cary. p 26

- December 1785. William BROADNAX and Sarah Jones of Bath Parish. Married by the Rev. Thomas Lundie, Rector of St. Andrew's Parish. Ministers' Returns p 347

23 July 1792. Uriah BROCK and Martha Harrison, 21. Sur. Benjamin Lashley. p 71

28 July 1794. Uriah BROCK and Silvia Huskey. Sur. William Huskey. Married by the Rev. Edward Dromgoole. p 81

9 November 1801. Edward B. BROOKING and Rebecca Ann Jackson, dau.
    Ann Jackson. Sur. Frederick Smith. Wit. Francis Brooking.
    Married 12 November by the Rev. Aaron Brown, Methodist. p 129

8 August 1805. Francis BROOKING and Ann H. Smith, dau. Frederick Smith
    who is surety. Wit. Edward Smith and John Wall. Married 10 August
    by the Rev. Hubbard Saunders. p 151

24 November 1800. John BROWDER and Susanna Miller. Sur. Jacob Miller.
    Married by the Rev. Henry Merritt. p 123

29 December 1786. Thomapson BROWDER and Tabitha Johnson. Sur. Joseph
    Browder. Married by the Rev. Thomas Lundie, Rector of St. Andrew's
    Parish. p 43

9 May 1793. Urias BROWDER and Mary Quarles, ward of William Quarles
    who is surety. Wit. Dennis Dailey. Married by the Rev. Peter
    Wynne who says "Polly". p 75

19 December 1778. Aaron BROWN and Elizabeth Harwell, ward of Samuel
    Harwell. Sur. Buckner Harwell. p 23

26 September 1796. Alexander BROWN and Jane Simmons, ward of Sterling
    Edmunds. Sur. Herbert Hill. p 91

17 November 1778. Arthur BROWN and Mary Turner, widow. Sur. Henry
    Turner. Wit. Elizabeth McLemore. Arthur Brown of North Carolina.
    p 20

23 November 1795. Davis BROWN and Martha Abernathy. Sur. John
    Abernathy. Married by the Rev. Aaron Brown, Methodist. p 88

- -   1791. Jesse BROWN and Mason Hardaway. Married by the Rev.
    Thomas Lundie, Rector of St. Andrew's Parish. Ministers' Returns
    p 360

24 February 1800. John BROWN and Elizabeth Davis. Sur. Benjamin Davis.
    Married 27 February by the Rev. Aaron Brown, Methodist. p 119

3 December 1804. Lewis BROWN and Fanny Duggar. Sur. Thomas Marks.
    p 148

- December 1786. Richardson BROWN and Rebecca Marks. Married by the
    Rev. Thomas Lundie, Rector of St. Andrew's Parish. Ministers'
    Returns p 350

23 December 1790. Rowley BROWN and Nancy Abernathy. Married by the
    Rev. Aaron Brown, Methodist. Ministers' Returns p 358

26 November 1807. Stephen BROWN and Betsey L. Johnson. Sur. John
    R. Williams. Wit. John Brown. Married by the Rev. Thomas Adams,
    Methodist. p 164

24 October 1803. Thomas BROWN and Martha L. Trotter, ward of Richard
    Trotter. Sur. Isham R. Trotter. p 143

Returned 4 February 1790. William BROWN and Elizabeth Upchurch.
Married by the Rev. John King, Baptist. Ministers' Returns p 357

3 April 1797. William BROWN and Elizabeth Lester. Sur. Thomas Lester.
Returned 18 May by the Rev. Peter Wynne. p 98

8 December 1802. William BROWN and Patsey Lucas, dau. Frederick Lucas.
Sur. William Rivers. Wit. Mary Edmunds. William Brown of Greensville County. Married by the Rev. Aaron Brown, Methodist. p 137

26 November 1804. Abraham BUFORD and Susan Ingram. Sur. Cannon J.
Green. Married by the Rev. John Jones, Methodist. p 148

3 February 1798. John BUGG and Sally Malone. Sur. George Malone.
Married 6 February by the Rev. William Creath. p 104

29 November 1804. John BUGG and Rebecca Seward, 21. Sur. William
Seward. p 148

30 May 1782. John BURCH and Polly Firth, dau. Thomas Firth who is
surety. p 28

12 August 1797. Edward BURCHETT and Polly Jackson. Married by the
Rev. Aaron Brown, Methodist. Ministers' Returns p 369

13 February 1809. Beverly B. BURDGE and Ann Jones, ward of Thomas
Jones. Sur. Robert Watson. Wit. Darvill Thompson. Married
16 February by the Rev. Peter Wynne. p 171

20 September 1774. Frederick BURDGE and Frances Brown. Sur. Beverly
Brown. Wit. John Bennet and Lewis Brown. p 16

11 January 1794. Frederick BURDGE and Betsey Kelly, 21. Sur. Samuel
Kelly. Wit. Giles Kelly. Married 16 January by the Rev. Aaron
Brown, Methodist. p 79

21 November 1810. Drury BURGE and Eliza C. Jones. Sur. George H.
Jones. Married 22 November by the Rev. Edward Dromgoole. p 177

10 December 1804. Thomas BURGE and Martha Bass. Sur. Benjamin Bass.
Married 20 December by the Rev. Hubbard Saunders who says Burge.
See Thomas Bridge. p 148

15 October 1787. Wood BURGE and Elizabeth Davis, dau. Hezekiah Davis.
Sur. Wood Jones. Married by the Rev. Thomas Lundie, Rector of
St. Andrew's Parish. p 46

July 1789 - July 1790. Baalam BURROW and Mary Woodward. Married by the
Rev. Thomas Lundie, Rector of St. Andrew's Parish. Ministers'
Returns. p 356

8 February 1797. Gray BURROW and Nancy Parham, 21. Sur. Batts Parham.
Wit. William Atkingson. Married 9 February by the Rev. Hubbard
Saunders. p 96

11 March 1790. Hutchins BURTON and Ann Mitchell. Sur. Henry Bailey. Wit. William Bailey. Married by the Rev. John King, Baptist. p 59

22 August 1809. Thomas BURTON and Patsey Jarrott. Sur. Zachariah Jarrott. See Thomas Berton. p 172

11 December 1800. Armistead BURWELL and Mary Turnbull, dau. Robert Turnbull. Sur. Thomas Turnbull. Married 13 December by the Rev. Henry Merritt. p 124

23 September 1776. Thomas Clement BUTTS and Sarah Hunt. Sur. Robert Rivers. p 17

8 December 1795. James BYRNE, Jr. and Sarah S. Haskins, ward of John Haskins. Sur. Alexander Brown. Wit. Jane Simmons. James Byrne, Jr. of Petersburg. p 88

- December 1786. John CAIN and Jensey Abernathy. Married by the Rev. Thomas Lundie, Rector of St. Andrew's Parish. Ministers' Returns p 350

20 April 1784. Marsdin CAIN and Sinah Saunders, dau. Edward Saunders, deceased. Sur. Ebbin Saunders. p 33

20 April 1784. Mordecai CAIN and Sinah Saunders. This is an error. Original bond says Morsdin Cain. See Morsdin Cain. Brunswick p 44

26 November 1785. Peter CAIN and Elizabeth Powell. Sur. Drury Dunn. Of Albermarle Parish. Married by the Rev. Thomas Lundie, Rector of St. Andrew's Parish. p 37

27 December 1785. Peter CAIN and Scotty Mitchell, widow of Thomas Mitchell; of Albermarle Parish. Married by the Rev. Thomas Lundie, Rector of St. Andrew's Parish. p 36

18 March 1788. David CALLAHAN and Mary Dawson, dau. Samuel Dawson. Sur. Mason Garrett. Wit David Callahan. p 49

28 February 1785. Henry CALLAS and Sarah Morris. Sur. Robert Morris. p 35

24 November 1800. Green CAMP and Sally Broadus, dau. Shipley Broadus. Sur. Mark Justice. p 123

16 January 1799. Jesse CAMP and Sally Wallace, 21. Sur. Balaam Wallace. Wit. Jesse Wallace. Married by the Rev. Hubbard Saunders. p 110

26 August 1793. John CAMP and Patsey Justice, of age. Sur. George Johnson. Wit. Isaac Ledbetter and Richard Howard. Married 30 August by the Rev. Edward Dromgoole. p 76

12 June 1793. Parsons CAMPBELL and Susanna Ezell, 21. Archibald Ezell
makes affidavit as to her age and is surety. Wit. Samuel Ezell.
Married 13 June by the Rev. Aaron Brown, Methodist. p 76

19 February 1752. Robert CAMPBELL and Mary Neal. Sur. Lewis Parham.
Wit. Joshua Hicks. p 1

14 December 1791. William CANADY and Rebecca Jordan, of age. Sur.
Bennett Goodrum. Wit. James Jordan and John Goodrum. Married
22 December by the Rev. Aaron Brown, Methodist, who says Canaday.
See William Kennedy. p 67

5 April 1786. William CANNADY and Betsy Pilkington. Sur. Richard
Pilkington. Married by the Rev. Thomas Lundie, Rector of St.
Andrew's Parish. See William Kennedy. p 38

20 March 1802. George CARDWELL and Elizabeth Hicks, dau. John Hicks.
Sur. Joseph Jackson. Wit. James Hicks. p 133

16 March 1790. John A. CARGILL and Rachel Lester, dau. Eliza Lester.
Sur. Whited Lester. Wit. Thomas Medley. Married by the Rev.
Thomas Lundie, Rector of St. Andrew's Parish. p 59

23 November 1801. Isaac CARPENTER and Winefred Brewer, 21. Sur. John
Carpenter. Returned 23 December by the Rev. Ira Ellis. p 129

24 March 1789. John CARPENTER and Rachel Brewer. Sur. James Brewer.
Married by the Rev. John King, Baptist. p 53

20 November 1806. Marshall CARPENTER and Jincey Saunders, dau. John
Saunders. Sur. Wyatt Parish. Married by the Rev. Hubbard Saunders.
p 158

26 December 1803. Richard CARPENTER and Ritter Rhea, 21. Sur. John
Seward. p 144

28 December 1795. William CARPENTER and Polly Manning. Sur. William
Manning. Wit. G. H. Baskerville. Married 31 December by the
Rev. Edward Dromgoole. p 89

17 December 1798. Willis CARPENTER and Tempy Wray, 21. Sur. Britain
Wray. Married by the Rev. Ira Ellis. p 109

- -   1786. James CARRELL and Salley Griffies. Married by the
Rev. John King, Baptist. Ministers' Returns p 349

8 March 1790. Patrick CARRINGTON and Fanny Johnson, consent of
William Johnson who is surety. Married by the Rev. Aaron Brown,
Methodist. p 59

- August 1785. Harris CARTER and Mary Butler of Albermarle Parish.
  Married by the Rev. Thomas Lundie, Rector of St. Andrew's Parish.
  Ministers' Returns p 345.

23 January 1754. John CARTER and Rebecca Stuart. Sur. James Jones of
  Surry County. p 2

30 March 1758. Joseph CARTER and Mary Roberson, under 21. Sur.
  Archibald Wager. p 4

7 July 1805. Richard CATE and Mary C. Threat. Married by the Rev. Peter
  Wynne. Ministers' Returns p 382

3 January 1803. Richard CATES and Nancy Potts, 21. Sur. William
  Hampton. p 139

25 January 1779. John (?) CAUDLE and Frances Hardaway. Sur. John
  Hardaway. See. William Caudle. p 21

25 January 1779. William (?) CAUDLE and Frances Hardaway. Sur.
  John Hardaway. See John Caudle. p 21

6 November 1784. William CAUDLE and Martha Hall, widow of James Hall.
  p 33

30 January 1778. Merritt CELEY and Obedience King, dau. Nathaniel
  King. Sur. Charles King. Wit. Cuddy Harrison. Double wedding:
  see Charles King. p 19

18 January 1797. James CHAMBLISS and Rebecca Atkinson, dau. William
  Atkinson. Sur. James Atkinson. Wit. John Meglamire. Married by
  the Rev. Aaron Brown, Methodist. p 95

24 December 1777. Joel CHAMBLISS and Mary Bailey, dau. Robert Bailey.
  Sur. Henry Chambliss. Wit. Thomas Williams and John Hill. p 18

3 January 1799. John CHAMBLISS and Jane Rideout, dau. William Rideout.
  Sur. Giles Rideout. Wit. William Andrews. p 110

24 January 1758. William CHAPMAN and Tabitha Wyche, widow, of St.
  Andrew's Parish. Sur. Richard Kello. William Chapman of Meherrin
  Parish. p 4

5 October 1759. William CHAPMAN and Ezabel (Isabel?) Kemp. Sur.
  Edward Roberson. Wit. William Cryer. p 6

11 March 1783. William CHAPMAN and Martha Williamson, dau. Charles
  Williamson. Sur. Benjaman Wall. p 30

31 December 1806. John W. CHARLES and Nancy Macklin, consent of John
  Elliott. Sur. Frederick Maclin. p 160

15 December 1798. Wyatt CHEATHAM and Polly Barker, dau. Burwell
  Barker. Sur. Berryman Ezell. Wit. John Bowles. Married 20
  December by the Rev. Balaam Ezell, Baptist. p 109

24 April 1797. John CHEELY and Fanny Short. See John Cheley.
Brunswick   p 48

24 April 1797. John CHELEY and Fanny Short, dau. John Short. Sur. Arad
Welton. Wit. John L. Wilkins. Married 11 May by the Rev. Aaron
Brown, Methodist. See John Cheely. p 98

21 December 1792. John CHILES and Loise Browder, "upward of 21". Sur.
Joseph Browder. Wit. Thomas Faulke. Married 22 December by the
Rev. Aaron Brown, Methodist, who says Lois. p 72

28 January 1798. Edward CHRISTIAN and Patsey Morris, 21. Sur. Sherod
Morriss. Wit. Susanna Singleton. p 104

July 1787 - July 1788. John CHRISTIAN and Oney Clements. Married by
the Rev. Thomas Lundie, Rector of St. Andrew's Parish. Ministers'
Returns p 352

12 November 1800. John CHRISTIAN and Sally Sills. Sur. Gregory
Hudson. Married by the Rev. John Neblett. p 123

14 September 1786. Richard CLACK and Anne Hardaway. Sur. Francis
Stainback. Married by the Rev. Thomas Lundie, Rector of St.
Andrew's Parish. p 40

3 June 1794. Richard CLACK and Amey Maclin, consent of Frederick Maclin.
Sur. Frederick Maclin, Jr. p 81

16 October 1757. William CLACK and Betty Twitty, under 21. p 4

14 September 1798. John CLAIBORNE and Sally Clayton. Sur. Philip
Claiborne. p 107

23 September 1802. John CLAIBORNE and Nancy Jones. Married by the
Rev. Aaron Brown, Methodist. Ministers' Returns p 385

25 November 1805. Thomas CLAIBORNE, Jr. and Hannah Hicks, 21. Sur.
Augustine Claiborne. p 153

27 September 1790. George CLANTON and Anne Wills. Sur. John Wills.
Married by the Rev. John King, Baptist. p 60

31 January 1783. Elisha CLARK and Mary Hardaway, widow. Sur. Lewis
Brown, Jr. p 30

16 January 1799. Thomas CLARK and Elizabeth Malone. Married by the
Rev. Peter Wynne. Ministers' Returns p 372

5 November 1806. John CLARKE and Elizabeth Murrell, 21. Sur. Clement
Mitchell. Married 7 November by the Rev. Aaron Brown, Methodist.
p 158

30 November 1799. Edwin CLARKE and Polly Thrower, dau. Christopher
Thrower. Sur. Solomon Cooke. Married 12 December by the Rev.
James Meacham. p 116

28 November 1786. Benjamin CLARY and Winifred Kelly. Sur. David
Kelly. Dau. Martha Kelly. Married by the Rev. John King,
Baptist. p 42

28 January 1788. John CLARY and Sarah Moseley. Sur. William Moseley.
Married by the Rev. John King, Baptist. p 49

10 December 1807. John CLARY and Middy Edmunds. Sur. William Linch.
Married 16 December by the Rev. Edward Dromgoole. p 165

27 November 1786. Thomas CLARY and Sarah Moseley. Sur. Peter Read.
p 41

19 January 1779. John CLAY and Patty Ingram, dau. John Ingram who
consents. Sur. Moses Ingram. p 21

26 November 1776. John CLAYTON and Temperance Hill, dau. G. Hill who
consents. Sur. Peter Pelham, Jr. Wit. Charles Stewart, Joseph
Peebles, William Brickett and William Hill. p 17

27 December 1790. John CLAYTON and Sarah Harris, 21. Sur. Charles
Harris. Wit. Sterling Peebles and William Atkinson, Jr. Returned
20 January 1791 by the Rev. Aaron Brown, Methodist. p 62

13 December 1800. William CLAYTON and Mary (Polly) Williams, dau.
Miles Williams. Sur. Richard Evans. Married 22 December by the
Rev. Peter Wynne. p 124

-   - 1787. John CLEATON and Mary Taylor. Married by the Rev. John
King, Baptist. Ministers' Returns p 253

28 April 1788. Thomas CLEATON and Anne Barner, dau. John Barner.
Sur. Thomas Washington. Wit. Wilson Walker. Married by the
Rev. John King, Baptist, who says Betsy Ann Barner. p 50

2 December 1772. Thomas CLEMENTS and Amy Maclin, dau. John Maclin.
Sur. William Edwards. p 12

10 February 1790. Richard CLOUGH and Jane Thornton, consent of
William Thornton. Sur. Sterling C. Thornton. Married by the
Rev. Aaron Brown, Methodist. p 58

17 December 1787. Abraham COCKE and Anne Hardy, dau. Richard Hardy.
Sur. Benjamin Whitehead. Married 21 December by the Rev. John
King, Baptist. p 48

4 May 1769. Peter COCKE and Mary Whitehead, dau. Richard Whitehead,
who is surety. Wit. Jeames Whitehead. p 7

21 March 1775. Thomas COCKE and Elizabeth Willis. Sur. Richard
Peete. p 17

23 July 1754. William COCKE and Rebecca Edwards. Sur. Nathaniel
Edwards. p 2

24 March 1772. William COCKE and Mary Maclin, dau. William Maclin who consents. Sur. William Thornton. Wit. William Maclin. p 11

1 November 1806. Jesse COE and Selah D. Gilliam, ward of William Mason. Sur. Aaron Brown. Married 5 November by the Rev. Aaron Brown, Methodist, who says Celia. p 158

23 December 1808. Richard COLEMAN and Dorothy Atkinson. Sur. Herbert Hill. Wit. John Phipps. p 169

29 January 1810. Williamson COLEMAN and Martha Burdge. Sur. Wesley Burdge. p 174

28 January 1803. Abram COLEY and Sarah Hightower. Married by the Rev. Peter Wynne. Ministers' Returns p 380

16 December 1799. Benjamin COLLIER and Middleton Brewer, dau. Jesse Brewer. Sur. Thomas Nolan. Married 19 December by the Rev. Edward Dromgoole. p 116

5 September 1787. Edmund COLLIER and Anne Washington, dau. Sarah Washington who consents. Sur. Joseph Browder. Wit. Thomas Washington and Gary Washington. Married by the Rev. Thomas Lundie, Rector of St. Andrew's Parish. p 45

6 January 1796. Edmund COLLIER and Judith Hicks, dau. John Hicls. Sur. Spain Marshall. Wit. Nancy Hicks and William Cordle. Married 7 January by the Rev. Aaron Brown, Methodist. p 90

23 November 1807. Henry COLLIER and Milly Britt. This is an error. The original bond says Henry Cotton. Brunswick p 52

3 October 1792. Ingram COLLIER and Susanna Browder, 21. Joseph Browder gives affidavit as to her age. Sur. Edmund Collier. Married 4 October by the Rev. Aaron Brown, Methodist. p 71

30 October 1797. Miles COLLIER and Nancy Gee, 21. Sur. Joshua Gee. Wit. John Gee. Married by the Rev. Aaron Brown, Methodist. p 100

1 August 1769. Moses COLLIER and Nancy Blank. Sur. John House. Wit. John Maclin, Jr. p 7

26 November 1769. Myhill COLLIER and Tabitha Harrison, dau. Benjamin Harrison. Sur. Charles Collier. Wit. Reuben Booth. p 7

17 September 1802. Nathaniel COLLIER and Salley Williamson, 21 Sur. Herbert Hill. Wit. Wright Tucker and Charlotte E. Williamson. Married 22 September by the Rev. Wright Tucker, Episcopal Rector. p 135

22 November 1773. William COLLIER and Patty (Martha) Thweatt, dau. Miles Thweatt, Jr., deceased. Richard Stewart guardian of Martha and Burwell Thweatt the two children of Miles Thweatt, Jr. Sur. John Jones. Wit. Frederick Collier and Frederick Rives. p 14

20 December 1781. Capt. William COLLIER and Mary Gee, dau. William
     Gee. Sur. John Gee. Wit. Lewis COLLIER and Frederick Collier. p 27

19 January 1791. William Smith COLLIER and Patsey Atkinson, dau.
     William Atkinson. Sur. John Sturdivant. Wit. Sarah Atkinson and
     Thomas Atkinson. Married by the Rev. John King, Baptist. p 63

20 May 1802. William Smith COLLIER and Sally Watson. Sur. Green
     Jackson. Married by the Rev. James Meacham. p 134

18 March 1790. William CONALLY and Sally Fort. Married by the Rev.
     Aaron Brown, Methodist. Ministers' Returns p 358

30 October 1807. Robert CONNELL and Anna Smith, dau. Eli and Mary
     Smith. See Robert Cornel and Robert Connelly. Brunswick p 52

31 December 1799. Daniel CONNELLY and Elizabeth King, dau. Charles
     King. Sur. Miles King. Wit. Ann King. Married by the Rev.
     Peter Wynne. p 117

22 May 1803. Lewis CONNELLY and Lucy Alley, 21. Sur. William Turbyfill.
     Married 30 May by the Rev. Edward Dromgoole. p 140

4 November 1807. Robert CONNELLY and Anne Smith. Married by the Rev.
     Aaron Brown, Methodist. See Robert Cornell and Robert Connell.
     Ministers' Returns p 387

17 March 1790. William CONNELLY and Sally Fort, 21, dau. Martha Fort.
     Sur. Miles Williams. Wit. Benjamin Evans and Robert Johnson.
     Married by the Rev. Aaron Brown, Methodist. p 59

16 August 1796. Charles COOCEY and Sarah King, dau. Nathaniel King, Sr.
     Sur. Walter Coocey. Wit. Nathaniel Edwards. Married 18 August
     by the Rev. Aaron Brown, Methodist. p 91

21 September 1759. John COOK and Betty Brown. Sur. John Peterson.
     Wit. Batt Peterson and Mark Jackson. John Cook under 21, son of
     Henry Cook. p 6

3 January 1793. Hezekiah COOKSEY and Ann Rivers, dau. John Peebles and
     Ann Peebles (Step-dau.?). Sur. Robert Rivers. Wit. John Rideout,
     William Andrews and John Green. p 74

July 1790 - July 1791. Edmund COOPER and Patsy Jackson. Married by the
     Rev. Thomas Lundie, Rector of St. Andrew's Parish. See Edward
     Cooper. Ministers' Returns p 359

- November 1790. Edward COOPER and Patsey Jackson. Sur. William
     Edward Broadnax. Wit. John Jones and Hartwell Tucker. See
     Edmund Cooper. p 62

20 February 1794. Isaac COPPEDGE and Sarah Jackson, 21. Sur. Moses
     Lansford. Wit. Daniel Mourning. Married 22 February by the Rev.
     Aaronb Brown, Methodist. p 79

22 December 1800. Charles CORDLE and Tabitha Harrison. Sur. Herbert
Hill. Wit. G. Wynn. Married 29 December by the Rev. James
Meacham. p 125

30 October 1807. Robert CORNELL and Anna Smith, dau. Ely and Mary
Smith. Sur. Daniel Smith. See Robert Connell and Robert
Connelly. p 164

23 November 1807. Henry COTTON and Milly Britt. Sur. Abner Woolsey.
Married 9 December by the Rev. Edward Dromgoole. See Henry
Collier. p 164

26 March 1793. Thomas COTTON and Sarah Hall, over 21. Sur. George
Johnson. Wit. Mordecai Howard and Joseph Atkins. Married
27 March by the Rev. Edward Dromboole. p 75

14 October 1756. Dr. Clack COURTNEY and Prudence Clarke, dau. George
Clarke who is surety. p 3

23 December 1782. Washington CRAFT and Polly Berry, dau. George Berry,
deceased. Sur. Gardner Scoggin. p 29

22 October 1792. Washington CRAFT and Mary Tilman, 21. William Parham
gives affidavit as to her age. Sur. William Parham. Wit. Martha
Edwards and John Tilman. p 72

Returned 4 February 1790. William CRENSHAW and Sarah Hight. Married
by the Rev. John King, Baptist. Ministers' Returns p 357

31 May 1802. James CRICHTON and Salley Winfield. Sur. Edward Winfield.
p 134

24 May 1798. Earby (Irby?) CROOK and Sally Traylor. Married by the
Rev. Peter Wynne. Ministers' Returns p 368

26 May 1800. Giles CROOK and Sarah Ward Kelly, dau. Samuel Kelly. Sur.
Joshua Lucy and Lues (Lewis?) Kelly. Married 3 June by the
Rev. Aaron Brown, Methodist. p 121

23 December 1793. James CROOK and Fanny Robinson. Sur. Christopher
Robinson. Married 24 December by the Rev. Aaron Brown, Methodist.
p 78

24 May 1790. John CROOK and Rebecca Nash, of age, dau. John Nash.
Samuel Kelley makes affidavit as to her age. Sur. Joshua Lucy.
Wit. George Crook. Married 9 June by the Rev. Aaron Brown,
Methodist. p 60

21 January 1783. Joseph CROOK and Elizabeth Derry, dau. George Berry,
deceased. Sur. William Connolly. p 30

4 December 1806. Joseph CROOK and Elizabeth G. Collier. Sur. Robert
Mitchell. Married by the Rev. Aaron Brown, Methodist. p 159

26 January 1808. Robert CROOK and Sally McKenny, dau. James McKenny. Sur. Young D. Perkins. Wit. Gideon Perkins. p 166

23 July 1770. Richard CROSS and Anne Maclin, dau. William Maclin. Sur. William Clack. Wit. Matthew Parham, Jr., and Ambrose Gresham. p 9

26 February 1803. John CROW and Martha Briggs, 21. Sur. Richard Briggs. Married 2 March by the Rev. John Rogers. p 140

26 November 1805. Bartholomew CROWDER and Jane C. Thompson, 21, ward of J. M. Thompson. Sur. John Bishop. Wit. Miles Crowder. p 152

Returned 4 February 1790. Larkin CROWDER and Lucy Rattenburg. Married by the Rev. John King, Baptist. Ministers' Returns p 357

8 November 1804. Miles CROWDER and Elizabeth B. Thompson, 21. Sur. Robert Blackwell. Wit. John Bishop and Elizabeth Bishop. p 147

7 December 1795. Thomas CROWDER and Mary Jordan. Sur. John Jordan. Wit. Frederick Tucker. p 88

16 January (no year given) (1786). William CROWDER and Phebe Elder. Sur. Thomas Grubbs. Married 1786 by the Rev. John King, Baptist. p 52

July 1790 - July 1791. William CULLAN and Darcus Steagall. Married by the Rev. Thomas Lundie, Rector of St. Andrew's Parish. See William Cullom. Ministers' Returns p 359

1 February 1791. William CULLOM and Darcus Steagall. Sur. Samuel Steagall. See William Cullan. p 64

12 October 1795. Richard CURD and Nancy Harrison, 21. Sur. Theophilus Harrison. Wit. Benjamin Harrison. Married 14 October by the Rev. Aaron Brown, Methodist. p 87

20 January 1801. James D - and Lucy Walker. Married by the Rev. James Meacham. Ministers' Returns p 378

18 October 1799. Andrew DAILEY and Huldy Collins. Sur. Michael Tarwater. p 114

24 April 1797. Arthur DAILEY and Jane Parrish. Sur. Thomas Parrish. Married 10 May by the Rev. James Meacham. p 98

7 August 1788. Denice DAILEY and Mildred Smith. Sur. Theophilus Harrison. Wit. Edmund Collier and Gray Washington. Married by the Rev. Thomas Lundie, Rector of St. Andrew's Parish who says Dennis Dailey. p 50

9 September 1788. Alexander DAMERON and Becky Lightfoot. Sur. Charles Dameron. Dau. Henry and Mary Lightfoot. Married by the Rev. Thomas Lundie, Rector of St. Andrew's Parish. p 50

11 December 1787. Thomas DANCE and Sarah Fisher, dau. James Fisher, deceased. Sur. Johnathan Fisher. Married by the Rev. Thomas Lundie, Rector of St. Andrew's Parish. p 48

9 September 1779. Francis DANCEY and Sarah Turner (widow). Sur. James Mason. Wit. John Turner and Martha Wilson. p 22

15 December 1797. George DANIEL and Armon Brown, dau. William Brown. Sur. Alexander Daniel. Wit. Green Jackson and Maryan Brown. p 101

15 January 1798. Joseph DANIEL and Sally Cordle, 21. Sur. John Barrow. p 103

23 December 1806. Hezekiah DANIEL and Nancy Tarpley, 21. Sur. Randolph Slate. Married 25 December by the Rev. Aaron Brown, Methodist. p 159.

7 January 1791. Robert DANIEL and Martha Hawks, 21. Sur. Randolph Steagall. Wit. Wylie Harrison. Married 13 January by the Rev. John Rogers. p 63

31 January 1807. William R. DANIEL and Polly Barrow. Sur. John Barrow. Married by the Rev. Aaron Brown, Methodist. p 161

11 November 1801. Allen W. DAVIS and Priscilla Gee. Sur. Daniel Hay-More. Married 12 November by the Rev. Aaron Brown, Methodist. p 129

19 May 1802. Edward DAVIS and Elizabeth Boswell. Sur. Thomas S. Bailey. Wit. William Boswell. Married 24 May by the Rev. Aaron Brown, Methodist. p 133.

4 October 1803. Holland DAVIS and Polly Bruce, dau. James Bruce. Sur. Joseph Saunders. Married 13 October by the Rev. Hubbard Saunders. p 142

16 January 1801. James DAVIS and Lucy Walker, 21. Sur. David Walker. Married 20 January by the Rev. James Meacham. p 125

4 February 1796. John DAVIS and Frances Collier. Sur. Charles Collier. Married 18 February by the Rev. Aaron Brown, Methodist. p 90

28 August 1798. John DAVIS and Elizabeth Howerton, of age. Sur. Drury Howerton. Wit. Nathaniel Harper. Married 9 September by the Rev. Peter Wynne. p 106

8 December 1798. John DAVIS and Jane Abernathy, dau. John Abernathy, Sr. Sur. Absolom Harwell. Returned 31 January 1799 by the Rev. Peter Wynne. p 108

31 October 1782. Joseph DAVIS and Sarah Wright. Married by Rev. John King, Baptist. Returned 17 January 1783. Ministers' Returns p 345

26 March 1770. Joshua DAVIS and Ann Smith. Sur. Cuthbert Smith. p 8

9 June 1795. Lewis DAVIS and Bridgett Gee. Sur. William Gee. Married 11 June by the Rev. Aaron Brown, Methodist. p 86

22 March 1773. Matthew DAVIS and Tabitha Tuell. Sur. Lawrence House. p 13

27 January 1803. Slayton DAVIS and Polley Ingram, of age. Sur. John Turbyfill. Married by the Rev. Aaron Brown, Methodist. p 139.

20 December 1802. Sterling DAVIS and Rebecca Caudle, 21, consent of Z.(?) Davis. Sur. Robert Hall. Married 25 December by the Rev. Hubbard Saunders. p 138

28 August 1769. William DAVIS and Agnes Lanier, dau. William Lanier, who consents and is surety. Wit. Augustine Willis. p 7

16 January 1756. Samuel DAWSON and Martha Jones, dau. Thomas Jones who is surety. Wit. Ben Chapman. Samuel Dawson of Amelia County. p 2

27 March 1798. Jesse DAY and Elizabeth Hearn, dau. John Hearn, Sr. Sur. John Hearn, Jr. Wit. Nancy B. Hearn. Married 29 March by the Rev. Balaam Ezell. p 104

13 January 1794. Lewis DAY and Polly Lanier, 21. Sur. Ephraim Jackson. Wit. Henry Mangum. Married 16 January by the Rev. Edward Dromgoole. p 79

24 November 1800. Robert DEAN and Patty Clements. Sur. Henry Jones. p 123

25 April 1759. George DEARDEN and Martha Burch, ward of Richard Burch who consents. Sur. William Thornton. Wit. Richard Burch, Jr. p 5

26 October 1789. John DELANY and Sarah Ingram. Sur. Jehu Adkins. Married by the Rev. Thomas Lundie, Rector of St. Andrew's Parish. p 55

22 May 1803. Benjamin DELBRIDGE and Sally Jackson, dau. Ephraim Jackson. Sur. Joshua Mitchell. Returned 16 June by the Rev. Ira Ellis. p 140

28 May 1804. Thomas DELBRIDGE and Sally Woolsey. Sur. Abner Woolsey. Wit. Nancy Woolsey. Married 14 June by the Rev. Ira Ellis. p 146

11 May 1753. Henry DELONG and - Walker, widow. Sur. John Maclin. Wit. John Parrish. See Henry Delony. p 1

11 May 1753. Henry DELONY and Rebecca Walker, widow of Alexander Walker. Nee' Broadnax. Henry Delony of Lunenburg County. Sur. John Maclin. See Henry Delong. Brunswick p 58

25 October 1796. Benjamin DENTON and Mary Manning. Sur. Caleb Manning. Wit. Thomas Manning. Married 27 October by the Rev. Aaron Brown, Methodist. p 92

14 April 1802. John DERBY and Lucy Porter. Sur. John Porter. p 133

7 January 1796. David DISMANG and Elizabeth Tilley, 21. Sur. John
     Tilley. Wit. Joseph Seward. Married 8 January by the Rev.
     Edward Dromgoole. p 90

Returned 4 February 1790. James DISMAY and Dolley Wright. Married by
     the Rev. John King, Baptist. Ministers' Returns p 357

24 September 1794. William DISMONG and Sally Hulmn. Married by the
     Rev. Peter Wynne. In a duplicate entry the bride's name is
     spelled Huluise. Ministers' Returns p 363

28 January 1799. John DIXON and Rebecca Abernathy, ward of John
     Abernathy. Sur. Miles Abernathy. Wit. Israel Maris. Married
     7 February by the Rev. Aaron Brown, Methodist. p 111

July 1789 - July 1790. Tilman DIXON and Mary Carlos. Married by the
     Rev. Thomas Lundie, Rector of St. Andrew's Parish. This bond is
     in Sussex County. Ministers' Returns p 356

23 August 1802. Bowler DOBBINS and Jane Hearn. Sur. John Hearn.
     Married 9 September by the Rev. Ira Ellis. Brunswick says Ann
     Hearn which is an error; the original bond gives Jane. p 135

12 August 1802. Thomas DRAKE and Caty Vaughan, 21. Joshua Vaughan
     makes affidavit as to her age. Sur. Joshua Vaughan. Wit. William
     Turbyville. Married by the Rev. Aaron Brown, Methodist. p 134

5 March 1777. Edward DROMGOOLE and Rebecca Walton. Sur. John Walton.
     p 17

10 December 1791. John DRUMMOND and Katharine Love. Sur. Allan Love.
     Wit. James Hand (?). Married by the Rev. Thomas Lundie, Rector
     of St. Andrew's Parish who says Catharine. p 67

28 January 1806. James W. DRUMRIGHT and Elizabeth Saunders, dau. Mary
     Saunders. Brunswick p 60

22 April 1799. Richmond DUGGAR and Elizabeth Crowder. Sur. Jesse
     Rainey. Married by the Rev. Aaron Brown, Methodist. p 112

27 February 1792. Henry DUGGAR and Armon Duggar, dau. Lurany Price.
     (Spelled Luvany when she married Joseph Price). Sur. Richardson
     Brown. Wit. Joseph Price and Howell Duggar. Married 1 March by
     the Rev. Aaron Brown, Methodist, who says Henry Dugger, Jr. p 70

21 December 1795. Howell DUGGAR and Polly B. Firth, 21. Sur. William
     Firth. Wit. John Duggar, Jr. Married 24 December by the Rev.
     Aaron Brown, Methodist, who says Mary. p 89

12 September 1787. James DUGGAR and Nancy Brown, 21, dau. Lewis Brown.
     Sur. Lester Morriss. Married by the Rev. Thomas Lundie, Rector
     of St. Andrew's Parish. p 46

24 January 1791. Jerman DUGGAR and Mary Raney, of age. Sur. Daniel
     Duggar. Wit. Richard Dugger and James Brown. Married by the
     Rev. Thomas Lundie, Rector of St. Andrew's Parish. p 63

14 December 1791. John DUGGAR and Nancy Edwards. Sur. Jesse Edwards.
     Wit. Edward Birchett. See James Dugger. p 67

4 September 1787. German DUGGER and Elizabeth Price, dau. Joseph
     Price who is surety. See Jerman Dugger. p 45

4 September 1791. James DUGGER and Nancy Edwards. See John Duggar.
     Brunswick p 60

24 December 1791. James DUGGER, Jr. and Nancy Edwards. Married by
     the Rev. Aaron Brown, Methodist. Ministers' Returns p 359

Between July 1787 and July 1788. Jerman DUGGER and Elizabeth Price.
     Married by the Rev. Thomas Lundie, Rector of St. Andrew's Parish.
     See German Dugger. Ministers' Returns p 351

7 April 1789. Sterling DUGGER and Sally Dugger. Sur. John Dugger.
     Married 8 April by the Rev. Aaron Brown, Methodist. p 54

15 April 1805. Robert DUNKLY and Nancy Barrow, dau. William Barrow.
     Sur. Dennis Barrow. Wit. Lewis Barrow. Married 18 April by the
     Rev. Aaron Brown, Methodist. p 150

23 March 1789. Thomas DUNN and Elizabeth Collier, over 21. Sur. Isaac
     Hicks. Wit. Myhill Collier. p 53

22 October 1788. Walter DUNNINGTON and Nancy Judd. Sur. John Judd.
     Married by the Rev. Thomas Lundie, Rector of St. Andrew's Parish.
     p 51

11 June 1807. William DUNNIVANT and Elizabeth Samford, of age, dau.
     Milly Samford. Sur. William Scarbrough. William Dunnivant of
     Prince Edward County. Married by the Rev. Aaron Brown, Methodist.
     p 162

15 February 1780. James DUPREE and Mary Adams, dau. Isaac Adams who is
     surety. Wit. David Adams. James Dupree son of John Dupree. p 24

12 December 1787. John DU PREE and Nancy Short. Married by the Rev.
     John King, Baptist. Ministers' Returns p 253

22 June 1778. Jacobus EARLY and Sally Wall. Sur. Daniel Call. p 19

17 September 1788. John EASTER and Mary Walker, widow of David Walker.
     Sur. Joseph Lyell. p 50

8 December 1781. Thomas EATON and Ann Stith, dau. Buckner Stith, Sr.
     who consents. Sur. Buckner Stith, Jr. Wit. Andrew Meade and
     Howell Eldridge. Thomas Eaton of North Carolina. p 27

26 November 1792. Upton EDMONDSON and Martha Hightower. Sur.
     Rawleigh Hightower. p 72

20 November 1805. Benjamin EDMUNDS and Martha Haskins, dau. Elizabeth Haskins. Sur. John D. Wilkins. Married 23 November by the Rev. Aaron Brown, Methodist. See Benjamin Edwards. p 152

31 December 1810. Richard EDMUNDS and Helen Wray Stuart. Sur. James Edmunds. p 178

28 April 1794. Samuel EDMUNDS and Betsy Saunders. Sur. Thomas Saunders. Married by the Rev. Aaron Brown, Methodist. p 80

28 November 1774. Sterling EDMUNDS and Ermine Simmons. Sur. John Flood Edmunds. p 16

25 November 1771. Thomas EDMUNDS and Sarah Eldridge. Sur. John Ballard, Jr. Wit. Benjamin Simmons. He was son of Col. Nicholas Edmunds of Sussex County and she was the daughter of Elizabeth Stith by her former husband Thomas Eldridge. Her will XX W (1) 205. p 10

25 November 1793. Wyatt EDMUNDS and Rebecca Beck. Sur. James Huff. Wit. John White. Married 5 December by the Rev. Edward Dromgoole. p 77

20 November 1805. Benjamin EDWARDS and Martha Haskins, dau. Elizabeth Haskins. See Benjamin Edmunds. Brunswick p 64

26 November 1810. Benjamin EDWARDS and Elizabeth Nanny, dau. Drury Nanny. Sur. Daniel Nanny. Wit. Milly Nanny. Returned 13 December by the Rev. Cary James, Methodist. p 177

25 March 1793. Burwell EDWARDS and Lucy Stuart, of age. Sur. Richardson Brown. Wit. James Dugger and Charles Rawlings. Brunswick says Stewart. Married by the Rev. Aaron Brown, Methodist. p 74

18 January 1786. David EDWARDS and Lucy Weathers, dau. Isaac Weathers. Sur. Lewis Brown. Married by the Rev. Thomas Lundie, Rector of St. Andrew's Parish who says Lucy Withers. p 38

15 May 1786. Gray EDWARDS and Elizabeth Ingram, widow of Moses Ingram. Sur. Washington Craft. Married by the Rev. Thomas Lundie, Rector of St. Andrew's Parish, Brunswick County. p 39

19 December 1792. Herbert EDWARDS and Charlotte Williams, dau. Lazarus Williams. Sur. Nathaniel Williams. Wit. Howell Allen and Mary Phips. Married 21 December by the Rev. Edward Dromgoole. p 72

21 March 1798. Herbert EDWARDS and Sarah Stainback. Sur. Thomas Edwards. Wit. Burrel Edwards. Married by the Rev. Aaron Brown, Methodist. p 104

12 May 1756. Hugh EDWARDS and Sarah Daniel, dau. Peter Daniel. Sur. John Daniel, Jr. Wit. Edward Goodrich. p 3

28 March 1798. Jesse EDWARDS and Betsey Williams. Sur. David Williams. Married 29 March by the Rev. Aaron Brown, Methodist. p 104

29 June 1785. John EDWARDS and Elizabeth Rainey, dau. William Rainey.
Sur. Lewis Brown. p 35

- February 1786. John EDWARDS and Temperance Parker of Surry County.
Married by the Rev. Thomas Lundie, Rector of St. Andrew's Parish.
Ministers' Returns p 348

14 March 1786. Lewis EDWARDS and Rachel Wright. Sur. George Wright.
Married 15 March by the Rev. John King, Baptist. p 38

10 October 1787. Nathaniel EDWARDS and Mary Tatum, dau. Paul Tatum,
deceased, and Ellener Tatum. Sur. Tilman Avery. Married by the
Rev. Thomas Lundie, Rector of St. Andrew's Parish. p 46

18 November 1807. Sampson EDWARDS and Polly B. Marks. Sur. Richardson
Brown. Married 19 November by the Rev. Aaron Brown, Methodist.
p 164

23 October 1798. Thomas EDWARDS and Elizabeth Hancocke, of age. Sur.
John Greene. Wit. Mark Greene. p 107

22 September 1806. Thomas EDWARDS and Sally Ingram. Sur. Benjamin
Ingram. Married 1 October by the Rev. Peter Wynne. p 157

26 January 1807. Thomas EDWARDS and Nancy Matthews, ward of Drury
Matthews. Sur. John Wyche. Wit. Elizabeth Walker. p 160

1 December 1771. William EDWARDS and Susanna Maclin. Sur. John Maclin,
Jr. Wit. Thomas Maclin. p 10

21 September 1808. William EDWARDS and Mary Shepperson. Married by
the Rev. Peter Wynne. Ministers' Returns p 389

22 August 1785. David ELDER and Polly Read, consent of Joseph Elder;
consent of William Read. Sur. Joel Briggs. Wit. Nancy Briggs.
Both of St. Andrew's Parish. Married by the Rev. Thomas Lundie.
p 35

23 January 1797. David ELDER and Polly Phillips, dau. Thomas Phillips.
Sur. Thomas Wade. Wit. Ephraim Jackson. Married 1 February by
the Rev. Aaron Brown, Methodist. p 96

27 December 1800. Jonathan ELDER and Patsey Seward. Sur. Joseph
Seward. Returned 4 January 1801, by the Rev. Balaam Ezell,
Baptist. p 125

- September 1785. Newman ELDER and Martha Tucker of Bath Parish.
Married by the Rev. Thomas Lundie, Rector of St. Andrew's Parish.
Minister's Returns p 345

12 March 1806. Peter ELDER and Tabitha Kirkland, 21. Sur. Richard
Kirkland. Married 13 March by the Rev. Hubbard Saunders. p 155

1 June 1785. Aristotle ELDRIDGE and Ann Lanier, dau. Buckner Lanier.
Sur. Thomas Saunders. Wit. Randol and Amy Robertson. p 35

27 May 1782. Howell ELDRIDGE and Martha Fisher, dau. James Fisher. Sur. Thomas Edmunds. p 28

26 November 1773. Rolfe ELDRIDGE and Susanna Walker, dau. George Walker. Sur. Peter Pelham, Jr. Wit. Courteny Walker and Mary Walker. p 14

25 July 1770. George ELLIOTT, Jr. and Mary Merriott, ward of Richard Elliott. Sur. William Murphy. Wit. William Stainback. p 9

July 1788 - July 1789. John ELLIOTT and Mildred Maclin. Married by the Rev. Thomas Lundie, Rector of St. Andrew's Parish. Ministers' Returns p 354

24 March 1788. William ELLIOTT and Mary Jameson. Sur. Griffin Stith. p 50

27 September 1776. Joseph ELLIS and Selah Jordan, of age, dau. Thomas Jordan. Sur. Batte Peterson. p 17

14 March 1807. James ELMORE and Polly Pritchett, 21. Sur. William Pritchett. Married by the Rev. Aaron Brown, Methodist. p 161

24 January 1791. Jesse ELMORE and Ann Brand, dau. Thomas **Brann**. Sur. James Brand. Wit. James Tarpley, John Tarpley, Vinson Brand, Jesse Turner and Herbert Hill. Jesse Elmore son of James Elmore of Charlotte County. p 63

23 November 1795. Richard EPPES and Sarah Mathis. Sur. James Mathis. Wit. Charles Mathis. Married 28 November by the Rev. John Jones, Methodist. p 87

27 December 1788. John ETTA and Mary King, dau. Henry King. Sur. Jesse Felts. p 52

13 January 1786. Francis EVANS and Elizabeth Wade, widow. Sur. Aramanus Abernathy. Married by the Rev. Thomas Lundie, Rector of St. Andrew's Parish, Brunswick County. p 38

3 December 1808. Francis EVANS and Eliza L. Bottom. Sur. William Marshall. Married by the Rev. Thomas Adams, Methodist. p 169

18 December 1810. David L. EVANS and Polly Wyche, 21. Sur. James Wyche. Married 19 December by the Rev. Cary James, Methodist. p 178

27 March 1803. John EVANS and Elanor Hughs Owen, 21. Sur. Nathaniel Morris. Wit. Nancy Owen. Married 6 April by the Rev. Wright Tucker, Episcopal Rector. p 140

21 December 1778. William EVANS and Rebecca Braten. Sur. William Wade. Wit. Laurance Asselin. p 20

22 December 1794. Davis EZELL and Nancy Davis, 21. Sur. John Davis. Wit. Washington Croft. Married 23 December by the Rev. Aaron Brown, Methodist. p 83

4 November 1797. Jeremiah EZELL and Susanna Ezell, consent of William
Ezell. Sur. Herbert Hill. Wit. Mical Ezell and Thomas Ezell.
Married 16 November by the Rev. Balaam Ezell, Baptist. p 100

30 July 1796. Thomas EZELL and Nancy Hill, dau. Charles Hill. Sur.
Herbert Hill. Married 3 August by the Rev. Balaam Ezell, Baptist.
p 91

- December 1786. William FEASON and Martha Hutchins. Married by the
Rev. Thomas Lundie, Rector of St. Andrew's Parish. Ministers'
Returns p 350

2 November 1791. William FEATHERSTON and Catharine Brann, dau. Thomas
Brann. Sur. James Brann. Wit. Vinson Brann. p 66

5 October 1803. James FENNELL and Betsy Hobbs, b. 1 December 1783,
dau. Hubbard and Martha Hobbs who consent. Sur. John Wyche. Wit.
John Hobbs, Jr. Married 26 October by the Rev. Ira Ellis. p 142

3 January 1799. Hutchins FERRELL and Mary Pennington. Sur. William
Pennington. p 110

3 January 1800. Hutchins FERRELL and Mary Pennington, dau. Anney
Pennington. Wit. William Pennington consent only. p 119

26 April 1790. Edmund FIELD and Mary Stith, dau. Drury Stith, deceased,
ward of Drury B. Stith. Sur. Edward Birchett. Married by the
Rev. Thomas Lundie, Rector of St. Andrew's Parish. p 59

15 June 1800. George FIELD and Elizabeth B. Stith, 21. Sur. David
Meade. Wit. Nancy W. Meade. Married 17 June by the Rev. Henry
Merritt. p 121

17 February 1794. Dr. Richard FIELD and Ann Meade, dau. Andrew Meade.
Sur. Richard Stith. p 79

3 June 1807. Dr. Richard FIELD and Sally Edmunds. Sur. Benjamin
Lewis. p 162

19 September 1783. Theophilus FIELD and Martha Simmons, widow. Sur.
Richard Elliott. Theophilus Field of Prince George County. p 31

29 December 1780. James FIELDING and Mary Slate, widow, dau. John
Davis. Sur. Thomas FIELDING. Wit. John Davis. p 25

30 August 1810. Edward FINCH and Jinsey Nanny. Sur. John Smith.
Married 3 September by the Rev. Cary James, Methodist. p 176

22 December 1789. George FINCH and Nancy Harrison Ivy, 21. Benjamin
Ivy, Sr. makes affidavit as to her age. Sur. Benjamin Ivy, Jr.
Wit. Charles Hicks. Married by the Rev. John King, Baptist, who
says Nancy Harrison. p 57

23 March 1801. William FINCH and Sally Moore, 21. Sur. John Moore.
Wit. Balaam Ezell. Married 25 March by the Rev. Balaam Ezell.
p 126

25 January 1796. William FIRTH and Nancy Crowder. Sur. John Duggar.
p 90

23 March 1796. William FIRTH and Sally Rawlings, 21, dau. Henry
Rawlings. Wit. Randolph Rawlings and John Rawlings. Married
24 March by the Rev. Aaron Brown, Methodist. p 90

28 December 1802. William FIRTH and Patsy Buchannan, 21, dau. of
Lindy Buchannan. Sur. Randolph Rawlings. Wit. Wright Griffin
and Robert Latimer. Married 30 December by the Rev. Hubbard
Saunders. p 138

28 October 1801. Benjamin FISHER and Nancy Dance. Sur. Herbert Hill.
p 128

1 October 1805. John FISHER and Ann Stith, consent of Richard Stith.
Sur. James Edmunds. Wit. Jane Stith and Edward O. Goodwyn. p 152

24 October 1799. Thomas D. FISHER and Sally North. Married by the
Rev. Peter Wynne. Ministers' Returns p 370

27 October 1806. William FISHER and Polly Cheely, consent of Joseph
and Winifred Cheely. Sur. John Chelly. Wit. Elizabeth Howell.
Married 6 November by the Rev. Peter Wynne. p 158

4 January 1790. Richard FITZHUGH and Susanna Meade, dau. Andrew Meade.
Sur. Griffin Stith. Married by the Rev. Thomas Lundie, Rector of
St. Andrew's Parish. p 58

18 December 1800. Richard FLETCHER and Elizabeth Jones. Married by
the Rev. Aaron Brown, Methodist. Ministers' Returns p 374

24 November 1800. Allen FLOYD and Sally L. Bottom, dau. John L. Bottom.
Sur. William L. Bottom. Married 26 November by the Rev. James
Meacham. p 123

29 October 1772. Charles FLOYD and Martha Davis, widow. Sur. Nathaniel
Roberson. Wit. Edward Thompson and Jane Thompson. p 12

16 January 1795. James FLOYD and Ann Nipper. Sur. Jesse Taylor. Wit.
Buckner Nipper. p 84

21 August 1802. Jordan FLOYD and Frances Capel, 21. Sur. Jesse
Sturdivant. Wit. Lewis Smith. p 134

9 November 1797. Morris FLOYD and Sally Floyd, 21. Sur. John Floyd.
Wit. William Floyd. p 100

7 December 1801. Wells FLOYD and Elizabeth Harrison, of age. Sur.
James Harrison. Wit. Thomas Washington. Married 10 December by
the Rev. James Meacham. p 130

10 November 1800. William FLOYD and Patsey Hammond. Married by the
Rev. John Neblett. Minister's Returns p 375

24 February 1772. Zachariah FLOYD and Anne Jones, dau. John Robert Jones who is surety. p 11

23 May 1796. Arthur FORT and Polly Finch, dau. William and Tabitha Finch. Sur. Edwin Fort. Wit. James Smith. Married 9 June by the Rev. Aaron Brown, Methodist. p 91

14 December 1799. Edward FORT and Lucy Lane. This is an error; the original bond is clearly Edwin Fort. See Edwin Fort. Brunswick p 72

14 December 1799. Edwin FORT and Lucy Lane, 21. Sur. Edmund Lane. Wit. Arthur Fort and Alexander Williams. Married by the Rev. Ira Ellis. p 116

23 April 1810. Beverly FOSTER and Nancy Ragsdale, of age. Sur. John Phipps. Married 9 March by the Rev. Cary James, Methodist. p 175

28 December 1795. John H. FOSTER and Celia Lightfoot. Sur. John Lightfoot. Married 31 December by the Rev. Edward Dromgoole. p 89

22 January 1798. John H. FOSTER and Sally Braswell, 21. Sur. William Ward. Married 25 January by the Rev. Edward Dromgoole. p 103

22 February 1803. Peter R. FOSTER and Sally James, dau. John P. James. Sur. John Braswell. Married 23 February by the Rev. Ira Ellis. p 140

8 February 1790. Briggs FOWLER and Molly Chambliss. Sur. James Pennington. Thomas Booth and Rachel Pennington. Married 15 February by the Rev. Aaron Brown, Methodist. p 58

7 December 1789. John FOWLER and Edith Tucker. Married by the Rev. Aaron Brown, Methodist. Minister's Returns p 355

11 December 1798. Miles FOWLER and Rebecca Redding, 21. Sur. Jesse Morris. Wit. Robert Lanier. Married 19 December by the Rev. Balaam Ezell, Baptist. p 108

10 December 1798. Mills FOWLER and Rebecca Redding. This is an error; the original bond says Miles Fowler. See Miles Fowler. Brunswick p 72

19 February 1805. Lark FOX and Elizabeth Gholson, dau. Thomas Gholson. Married 20 February by the Rev. Hubbard Saunders. Sur. Benjamin Gholson. p 150

24 December 1810. John FRASER and Martha Brown. Sur. Aaron Brown. p 178

25 November 1783. Arthur FREEMAN and Nancy Malone. Sur. James Johnson. p 31

- June 1786. Arthur FREEMAN and Susanna Courtney. Married by the Rev. Thomas Lundie, Rector of St. Andrew's Parish. To Arthur Freeman's name "Winfield" has been added later. Ministers' Returns p 348

31 January 1797. Hamlin FREEMAN and Betsey Hartwell, of age. Sur. Herbert Hill. Wit. Andrew Tarver and Harrison Hartwell. Married 2 February by the Rev. Aaron Brown, Methodist. p 96

24 January 1774. Hartwell FREEMAN and Elizabeth Bailey, dau. Robert Bailey. Sur. William Clack. Wit. John Russell. p 15

30 October 1787. Edward FURGASON and Elizabeth Hunter, dau. Margaret Sweet. Sur. Isaac Roe Walton. Wit. William Allen. p 47

27 May 1771. Samuel GARLAND and Elizabeth Edmunds, dau. Nicholas Edmunds. Sur. Sterling Edmunds. p 9

27 March 1786. Presley GARNER and Betsy Avent. Sur. William Avent. p 38

28 March 1780. William GARNER and Lucy Johnston, dau. James Johnston. Sur. William Goodrum. p 24

26 March 1787. William GARNER and Mary Samford. Sur. William K. Samford. Married in April 1787 by the Rev. Thomas Lundie, Rector of St. Andrew's Parish. p 44

26 October 1799. Humphrey GARRETT and Susanna Pritchett, 21. Sur. William Roberts. Wit. Samuel Bagwell. Married 28 October by the Rev. John Neblett. p 114

2 May 1789. Mason GARRETT and Winifred Beckwith Miskell, born 17 January 1768, dau. Daniel and Ann Miskell. Sur. John Miskell. Married by the Rev. Thomas Lundie, Rector of St. Andrew's Parish. p 54

- December 1802. Jonathan GEE and Jinsey Wells. Married by the Rev. Peter Wynne. Ministers' Returns p 380

14 April 1794. Lucas GEE and Lucy Pennington, dau. S. - Pennington. Sur. Benjamin Bugg. Wit. Asa Gresham. p 80

13 December 1801. William GEE and Susan Atkins, dau. Richard and Rebecca Atkins. Sur. William Wills. Married by the Rev. Peter Wynne who says Susanna Adkins. p 130

22 December 1808. Wilson GEE and Rebecca Turbefill. Sur. John Gee. Brunswick says Turbyfield. p 169

31 August 1769. Thomas GHOLSON and Jeanny Perry, 21. Sur. Mack Jackson. Wit. William Denton and Lucy Denton. p 7

3 May 1798. William GHOLSON and Mary Saunders. Sur. Herbert Hill. Married 9 May by the Rev. Aaron Brown, Methodist. p 105

6 July 1780. Edward GIBBONS and Mary Maclin. Sur. Ben Goodrich. Wm. & M.Q. 1st Ser. Vol. XX p 196: 1911

23 January 1804. John GIBBS and Patsey Wray. Sur. Baxter Wray. Married 28 January by the Rev. Ira Ellis. p 145

7 November 1784. William GIBBS and Elizabeth Ward. Sur. James Wesson.
p 33

14 January 1801. John GILES and Sally Lanier. Sur. Robert Lanier.
Married by the Rev. Balaam Ezell, Baptist. p 125

11 October 1798. Thomas GOLLEY and Susanna Evans. Married by the
Rev. Aaron Brown, Methodist. Ministers' Returns p 368

31 March 1785. John GOODE and Martha Simmons, widow. Sur. Andrew
Meade. Wit. Thomas Lundie and Lucy Lundie. p35

25 May 1789. Benjamin GOODRICH and Tabitha Hicks. Sur. Robert
Rivers. Married by the Rev. John King, Baptist. p 54

20 November 1799. Benjamin GOODRICH and Nancy S. Claiborne, 21. Sur.
William Warwick. Wit. John Walton and Thomas Goodrich. Benjamin
Goodrich ward of J. Goodrich, brother. p 115

3 February 1807. Edmund GOODRICH and Elizabeth B. Goodrich, 21. Sur.
Thomas Goodrich. Married 4 February by the Rev. Edward Dromgoole.
p 161

4 March 1800. Thomas GOODRICH and Elizabeth Warwick. Sur William
Warwick. p 120

23 November 1801. James GOODRUM and Polly Justice, 21. Sur. John
Carpenter. Returned 31 December by the Rev. Ira Ellis. p 129

27 November 1797. John GOODRUM and Rebecca Parham, 21. Sur. Mordecai
Jones. Wit. Ebbin Sanders. p 101

30 December 1781. Thomas GOODRUM and Jane Johnson. p 27

29 March 1780. William GOODRUM and Hannah Connally, dau. William
Connally. Sur. Bennett Goodrum. p 24

25 December 1797. John GOODWIN, Jr. and Lucy Green, 21, dau. Dolly
Green. Sur. John Green. Wit. Cannon Greer. p 102

19 December 1803. Càpt. Armistead GOODWYN and Sarah Dance, 21. Sur.
Nathaniel Collier. Wit. Susanna Fisher. Capt. Goodwyn of Greens-
ville County. Married 24 December by the Rev. Wright Tucker,
Episcopal Rector. p 143

27 April 1789. Esau GOODWYN and Patsy C. Tucker, dau. David Tucker.
Sur. Sterling Tucker and Hartwell Tucker. Married by the Rev.
Aaron Brown, Methodist. p 54

25 October 1791. John GOODWYN and Anne Collier, dau. William Collier.
Sur. James Peterson. Wit. William Gee. p 66

28 September 1787. Abner GORDON and Rebecca Ivie, dau. William Ivie.
Sur. Benjamin Ivie. Married by the Rev. John King, Baptist, who
says Ivey. p 46

4 January 1810. Moses GRANGER and Sally Ship. Married by the Rev.
     Peter Wynne. Ministers' Returns p 389

6 June 1809. William GRAVES and Martha Smith. This is an error; the
     original bond says Williamson Graves. See Williamson Graves.
     Brunswick p 76

6 June 1809. Williamson GRAVES and Martha Smith. Sur. Giles Rideout.
     p 172

13 October 1786. William GRAY and Mary Ledbetter, dau. Henry Ledbetter.
     Sur. David Hyde. William Gray of Southampton County. p 40

25 September 1786. Alexander GREEN and Sarah Atkins, dau. John Atkins,
     deceased, and Sarah Atkins, Sr. who consents. Sur. Charles Atkins.
     Parham Atkins also gives consent. Married by the Rev. John King,
     Baptist. p 40

14 February 1783. Clement GREEN and Frances Parham, dau. William Parham,
     deceased. Consent of William Mason. Sur. Frederick Green. Wit.
     Mordecaii Jones, S. Gilliam and John Lands. p 30

25 January 1779. Frederick GREEN and Frances Crittenden. Sur. William
     Mitchell. Wit. Mark Crowder and Henry Crittenden. p 21

25 April 1781. James GREEN and Patsey or Betsey Bass, dau. Thomas Bass.
     Sur. Robert Mallory. Wit. James Bass and Nancy Bass. p 25

5 December 1772. John GREEN and Dolly Jones, dau. John Robin Jones.
     John Green of Amelia County. Sur. Francis Barner. Wit. Henry
     Clark and John Roberts. p 12

8 January 1799. John GREEN and Sally Harper. Married by the Rev.
     Peter Wynne. Ministers' Returns p 372

23 April 1792. Mark GREEN and Ann Barbar Claiborne, 21. Sur. Thomas
     Claiborne. Wit. John Doe. p 70

14 December 1797. Mark GREEN and Patsey Warwick, of age. Sur. John
     Green. Wit. John Walton. Married 21 December by the Rev. Aaron
     Brown, Methodist. Brunswick says Patsy Harwell which is an error.
     Patsey Warwick writes her own consent which is attached to original
     bond. p 101

3 June 1808. Myhill GREEN and Nancy Jackson. Sur. Henry Rose. Married
     by the Rev. Thomas Adams, Methodist. p 167

23 April 1810. Nathaniel GREEN and Lucy Richardson. Sur. Thomas
     Richardson. Married 10 May by the Rev. Cary James, Methodist. p 176

23 October 1786. Peter GREEN and Dolly Foster, dau. Anthony Foster.
     Sur. James W. Green. p 41

24 September 1787. Sterling GREEN and Amey Eaves. Sur. Jesse Freeman.
     Wit. Harmon Harrison and Buckner Eaves. p 46

- -   1779. Williamson GREEN and -   -. Brunswick p 76

26 January 1789. Joseph GREENHILL and Patsey Stainback. Sur. William
    Stainback. Married by the Rev. John King, Baptist. p 53

- November 1785. Lewis GREY and Edith Watson. Married by the Rev.
    Thomas Lundie, Rector of St. Andrew's Parish. Ministers' Returns
    p 346

25 December 1802. Charles GRIGG and Priscilla Cheely. Sur. Charles
    Cheely. Married by the Rev. Hubbard Saunders. p 138

22 June 1801. John GRIMES and Rebecca Miskell, of age, consent of
    Jeremiah Miskell. Sur. Hubbard Suanders. Married by the Rev.
    Hubbard Saunders. p 127

16 May 1793. Hickerson GRUBBS and Caty Hailey, dau. of Thomas Hailey,
    Sr. Sur. John Hailey. Wit. Richard Biggs. Married by the Rev.
    John Paup who says Hickman. p 75

19 December 1807. Dudley GUNN and Sarah Tillman. Sur. John Tillman.
    Married 24 December by the Rev. Edward Dromgoole. p 165

13 September 1797. Radford GUNN and Silvey Read. Sur. Peter Read.
    Married by the Rev. Balaam Ezell, Baptist, who says Silvia. p 99

12 May 1756. John HAGOOD, Jr. and Lucy Rollins or Rowlings, dau.
    William Rollins. Sur. William Harrison. Wit. Bramley Rawlings. p 3

11 April 1808. Richard HAGOOD and Sally R. Smith. Sur. Thomas Smith.
    Married by the Rev. Thomas Adams, Methodist. p 166

29 November 1781. Robert HAILEY and Polley Crook, dau. George Crook.
    Sur. Moses Dobbins. Robert son of Thomas Hailey. p 26

26 December 1796. Sterling HAILEY and Liddia Ross, of age, John and
    Mary Miskell make affidavit as to her age. Sur. William Trotter.
    p 94

26 December 1791. Thomas HAILEY and Nancy Vaughan. Sur. Hickerson
    Grubbs. Wit. Miles Williams and John Hailey. Married by the Rev.
    Thomas Lundie, Rector of St. Andrew's Parish. See Thomas Hayley.
    p 68

25 December 1799. James HALDANE and Rebecca Maclin. Married by the
    Rev. Aaron Brown, Methodist. Ministers' Returns p 372

28 May 1770. Henry HALEY and Letitia Hyde, 22, of North Carolina, dau.
    of Milly Hyde. Moses Johnson makes affidavit as to age. Sur.
    Edward Fisher. p 8

5 January 1775. Discon (or Dickson) HALL and Ann Hunt. Sur. Thomas
    Rivers. Wit. Wingfield Mason. This name is also spelled Dyson.
    See Dyson Hall. p 16

23 November 1778. Durham HALL and Frances Hicks, ward of Robert Hicks.
     Sur. Lewis Hicks. Wit. William Jones, Jr. p 20

5 January 1775. Dyson HALL and Ann Hunt. See Dison Hall. Brunswick
     p 80

22 November 1802. Edward HALL and Elizabeth Kelly, 21. Sur. Wyatt
     Nanny. Married 1 December by the Rev. Ira Ellis. p 137

22 February 1809. John HALL and Elizabeth Smith. Married by the Rev.
     Peter Wynne. Ministers' Returns p 389

20 March 1797. James HALSEY and Susanna Ingram. This is an error; it
     is James Holsey in the original bond. See James Holsey.
     Brunswick p 80

25 February 1791. William HAMLIN and Polly Ginnings Fowlks, dau. Thomas
     Fowlks. Sur. Bennett Goodrum. Wit. John Orgain, Joseph Browder
     and Herbert Hill. Married 26 February by the Rev. Aaron Brown,
     Methodist. p 64

19 March 1792. Mark HAMOUR and Tabitha Hamour, dau. John Hamour. Sur.
     John Taylor. Wit. Charles Martain. Married 25 April by the Rev.
     Aaron Brown, Methodist. p 70

13 December 1803. David HAMPTON and Elizabeth Browder, 21. Sur. John
     Browder. p 143

29 January 1807. Jeremiah HAMPTON and Elizabeth Allen, 21. Sur.
     William Allen. Married 31 January by the Rev. Peter Wynne. p 160

13 December 1800. William HAMPTON and Patsey Potts. Sur. Peter Potts.
     Wit. Jeremiah Hampton. p 124

27 February 1804. Francis HANCOCK and Martha James. Sur. John Wyche.
     p 145

15 December 1791. Henry HANCOCK and Dolly Rawlings. Sur. Richard Rice.
     Wit. Rebecca Parrish and Ann Foster. Married 22 December by the
     Rev. Aaron Brown, Methodist. p 67

24 October 1803. Henry Simmons HARDAWAY and Susan Lundie, dau. Lucy
     Lundie. Sur. Alexander F. Lundie. Wit. John Atkinson. Returned
     23 November by the Rev. Hubbard Saunders. p 142

2 April 1810. James H. HARDAWAY and Elizabeth M. G. Raines. Sur. James
     Booth. Wit. William Mason and Hugh Love. Married 4 April by the
     Rev. Edward Dromgoole. p 175

26 January 1774. John HARDAWAY and Mary Sexton. Sur. Joseph Lett.
     Wit. Lewis Brown. p 15

21 February 1788. John HARDAWAY and Elizabeth Maclin, dau. Col. Freder-
     ick Maclin. Sur. Thomas Stith, Sr. p 49

24 November 1783. Robert HARDAWAY and Sarah Hicks, dau. James Hicks, Sr. Sur. Isaac Hicks. Robert HARDAWAY of Dinwiddie County. p 31

- July 1785. Thomas HARDAWAY and Rebecca Powell, both of Albemarle Parish. Married by the Rev. Thomas Lundie, of St. Andrew's Parish. Ministers' Returns p 345

25 October 1784. Capt. William HARDAWAY, Jr. and Elizabeth Hicks, dau. James Hicks. Sur. John Hicks. Wit. Isaac Hicks. p 33

July 1789 - July 1790. William HARDAWAY and Anne Tucker. Married by the Rev. Thomas Lundie, Rector of St. Andrew's Parish. Ministers' Returns p 356

25 November 1793. Abram HARDING and Sylvia Price. Sur. Joel Price (father?). Wit. Howell Harris. p 78

3 February 1804. Charles HARDY and Sally J. Green, 21, dau. Dolly Greene. Sur. Cannon J. Greene. p 145

6 February 1809. Vincent HARDY and Sally Penn. Sur. Griffin Orgain. p 170

- January 1788. Bennet HARGROVE and Biddy Lambert. Married by the Rev. John King, Baptist. Ministers' Returns p 253

22 November 1784. Manning HARP and Betty Mitchell. Sur. William Tarpley. p 34

22 December 1794. Benjamin HARPER and Anna Matthis, dau. John Mathis. Sur. Matthew Mathis. Wit. Nathaniel Harper. Brunswick says dau. Mathew Mathis which is an error; the original bond says dau. John Mathis. p 83

25 August 1800. Benjamin HARPER and Nancy Ingram, dau. John Ingram. Sur. Thomas INgram. p 122

25 July 1794. George HARPER and Martha Holloway. Married by the Rev. Peter Wynne. Ministers' Returns p 363

July 1789 - July 1790. James Thweat HARPER and Betsy Holloway. Married by the Rev. Thomas Lundie, Rector of St. Andrew's Parish. Ministers' Returns p 356

21 December 1778. Joseph HARPER and Elizabeth Lambert, widow. Sur. Drury Mathis. Joseph Harper of Dinwiddie County. p 20

11 February 1797. Nathaniel HARPER and Polly Fisher, consent of Jonathan Fisher. Married 16 February by the Rev. Peter Wynne. Sur. James Fisher. p 96

17 April 1799. William Worsham HARPER and Patsey Colson Tucker. Married by the Rev. Peter Wynne. Ministers' Returns p 372

24 January 1803. Benjamin HARRIS and Martha Clayton. Sur. John
   Clayton. Married by the Rev. Aàron Brown, Methodist. p 139

13 December 1779. Bowler HARRIS and Nancy Kemp Goodrich. Sur. Briggs
   Goodrich. p 23

27 June 1774. Etheldred HARRIS and Elizabeth Warren, dau. Benjamin
   Warren. Sur. Moses Harris. p 15

16 July 1770. Gideon HARRIS and Rittah Warren, consent of Benjamin
   Warren. Gideon son of Nathan Harris. Sur. Edward Fisher.
   Wit. Elias Harris and John Warren. p 9

26 October 1809. Henry HARRIS and Mary M. Roper. Married by the
   Rev. Peter Wynns. Ministers' Returns p 389

23 November 1789. Howell HARRIS and Polly Goodrich. Sur. John Camp
   of Greenville County. Howell Harris of Greenville County. p 56

31 October 1804. Jacob HARRIS and Nancy Gary. Married by the Rev.
   Aaron Brown, Methodist. Ministers' Returns p 386

2 May 1780. James HARRIS and Christian Harrison. Sur. Willis Wills.
   Wm. & M.Q. 1st Ser. Vol XX p 196: 1911

July 1787 - July 1788. John HARRIS and Rebecca Abernathy. Married by
   the Rev. Thomas Lundie, Rector of St. Andrew's Parish. Ministers'
   Returns p 351

16 June 1801. Kinchen HARRIS and Mary J. C. Chapman, dau. J. H. Chapman. Sur. James McInvale. Married by the Rev. Ira Ellis. p 127

25 December 1809. Larkin HARRIS and Polly Lightfoot, 21. Sur. John
   Phipps. Married 28 December by the Rev. Cary James, Methodist.
   p 173

20 November 1793. Robert HARRIS and Elizabeth Seward Clayton, dau.
   John Clayton who is surety. Married 26 November by the Rev.
   Aaron Brown, Methodist. p 77

18 January 1802. Sterling HARRIS and Sylvia Lane, widow. Sur. Edmund
   Lane. Married 22 January by the Rev. Hubbard Saunders. p 132

26 March 1787. Benjamin Harrison and Patty Jones. Sur. Herod Clary.
   p 44

12 October 1795. Benjamin HARRISON and Sally Cole. Sur. Theophilus
   Harrison. Married 14 October by the Rev. Aaron Brown, Methodist.
   p 87

13 December 1802. Benjamin HARRISON and Silvia Bass. Sur. Edmund
   Bass. Wit. Abner Wilson. Married 23 December by the Rev. Aaron
   Brown, Methodist. p 137

25 April 1808. Benjamin HARRISON and Polly Lashly. Sur. George Hardaway. Married 3 May by the Rev. Edward Dromgoole. p 166.

26 May 1800. Charles HARRISON and Betsey Glandish, of age. Sur. Jones
Williams. Wit. Peter Williams, consent only. Married 11 June by
the Rev. Hubbard Saunders. p 121

25 May 1801. Charles HARRISON and Betsey Glandish. Sur. Peter
Williams. p 127

29 January 1778. Cuddy HARRISON and Elizabeth Harrison, dau. Arthur
Harrison. Sur. Gabriel Harrison. Wit. Charles Harrison. Arthur
spelled "Arter". p 18

31 December 1810. Gabriel HARRISON and Sally Short, 21. Sur. Holland
Davis. p 178

7 January 1786. Ishmael HARRISON and Elizabeth Gee, dau. William Gee.
Sur. Thomas Rives. Wit. John Gee. Both of Meherrin Parish.
Married by the Rev. Thomas Lundie, Rector of St. Andrew's Parish.
p 38

14 December 1779. John HARRISON and Cressy Steed, dau. Winefred Steed.
Sur. Mark Steed. p 23

5 November 1799. John HARRISON and Dorothy Hancock. Sur. Harrison
Hartwell. Wit. Armsted Hartwell. Married 7 November by the Rev.
Edward Dromgoole. p 115

24 November 1808. John HARRISON and Polly Hicks, 21. Sur. Dixon
Stainback. p 168

26 October 1807. Joseph HARRISON and Anthania Hancock. Sur. Green
Hill. Married 4 November by the Rev. Edward Dromgoole. Brunswick
says Authanico. p 163

1 September 1809. Mark HARRISON and Mary Olive Whitby, dau. Sally
Whitby. Sur. John Bottom (John Longbottom?). p 172

17 November 1794. Nathaniel HARRISON and Elizabeth White, dau. Blumer
White. Sur. Stephen White. Wit. John White. p 82

25 March 1799. Nathaniel HARRISON and Martha K. Broadnex, 21. Sur.
Herbert Hill. Wit. Frederick Smith. p 112

25 May 1801. Nathaniel HARRISON and Rebecca Cook, 21. Sur. Nicholson
Cook. Wit. A. Wesson and Joshua Standly. Married by the Rev.
James Meacham. p 127

13 November 1798. Peter HARRISON and Catharine Boswell, 21. Sur.
William Boswell. Wit. Levi Williams and John Harrison. Married
15 November by the Rev. Aaron Brown, Methodist. p 107

- January 1787. Robert HARRISON and Martha Baugh. Married by the Rev. Thomas Lundie, Rector of St. Andrew's Parish. Ministers' Returns p 350

17 November 1794. Robert HARRISON and Elizabeth White, dau. Blumer White. Va. Mag. Vol. XXVIII p 167; April 1920

24 May 1790. Theop's HARRISON and Mary Love, dau. Hugh Love. Sur. Thomas Washington. Married by the Rev. Thomas Lundie, Rector of St. Andrew's Parish who says Theophilus. p 59

24 May 1790. Thomas HARRISON and Mary Love, dau. Hugh Love. This is an error; the signature on the bond is Theo's Harrison. See Theop's Harrison. Brunswick p 86

7 May 1759. William HARRISON and Ann Major. Sur. John Edmondson. Wit. Ann Harrison and Henry Harrison. p 5

23 December 1782. William HARRISON and Elizabeth Boswell, widow. Sur. Lewis Scarbrough. p 29

26 March 1787. William HARRISON and Patty Jones. Married 5 April by the Rev. John King, Baptist. Brunswick p 84

27 November 1797. William HARRISON and Tabitha Parham, 21. Sur. Robert Brooks. Married 7 December by the Rev. Balaam Ezell, Baptist. Wit. James Harrison and Robert Brooks. p 100

2 March 1799. William HARRISON and Elizabeth Tilman, 21, dau. Mille Tilman (mother). Sur. John Tilman. Married 7 March by the Rev. James Meacham. p 111

5 January 1802. Willie HARRISON and Nelly Holloway, ward of Asa Holloway. Sur. Henry F. Power. Married 13 January by the Rev. James Meacham. p 132

26 December 1796. Armistead HARTWELL and Martha Gholson, dau. Thomas Gholson. Sur. Andrew Tarver. Married 29 December by the Rev. Aaron Brown, Methodist who says Patsy. p 95

24 February 1806. Littleberry S. HARTWELL and Sally Woodruff, 21. Sur. James Powell. Wit. Ed. Heartwell. Married 27 February by the Rev. William Dossey, Baptist who says Woodrough. p 155

5 August 1771. Richard HARTWELL and Susanna Stainback, dau. Francis Stainback who is surety. p 10

27 February 1775. John HARVEY and Patty Ivey. Sur. Thomas Ivey. p 17

25 January 1791. Rawleigh HARVEY and Rainey Brintle, dau. Thomas Brintle. Sur. Triford Harvey. Wit. Allen Brintle. Married by the Rev. Henry Ogburn. p 64

8 February 1788. Triford HARVEY and Sarah Brintle, 21. Sur. Arad Welton. Married by the Rev. Thomas Lundie, Rector of St. Andrew's Parish. p 49

22 November 1802. Abslem (Absalom?) HARWELL and Rebecca Williams. Sur. George Williams. Married 8 December by the Rev. Peter Wynne. p 137

27 July 1786. Francis HARWELL and ELizabeth Loftin, dau. John Loftin of Greensville County. Sur. James Smith. Married by the Rev. Thomas Lundie, Rector of St. Andrew's Parish. p 39

2 February 1784. Harbert HARWELL and Anne Westmoreland, dau. Thomas Westmoreland, deceased. Sur. Samuel Harwell. p 32

21 December 1803. Hartwell HARWELL and Temperance Edwards, 21. Sur. Frederick Maclin. p 144

16 November 1779. James HARWELL and Rebekah Barner, consent of John Barner. Sur. Henry Bishop. Wit. Elizabeth Barner and Tabitha Barner. p 22

24 December 1796. Nathaniel HARWELL and Susanna Westmoreland. Sur. Peter Williams. Wit. Jones Williams. p 94

16 April 1805. Richard HARWELL and Nancy Owen. Sur. James Harwell. Wit. Thomas Lundie. Married by the Rev. Hubbard Saunders. p 150

11 March 1808. Richard M. HARWELL and Mary Atkinson, 21, dau. Sarah Atkinson. Sur. James Parham. p 166

27 February 1804. Shadrack HARWELL and Anne Harrison. Sur. Cuthbert Harrison. Returned 4 May by the Rev. Wright Tucker, Episcopal Rector. p 146

27 February 1805. William HARWELL and Sally Hicks. Sur. James H. Hardaway. p 150

17 November 1796. Owen HASKINS and Catharine Dennis. Married by the Rev. Peter Wynne. Ministers' Returns p 366

11 February 1802. Robert HASKINS and Susan Edmunds, consent of Lucy Edmunds. Sur. Creed Haskins. Wit. John Paup. p 132

27 December 1791. Smart HAWKINS and Marian Fort. Sur. William Connelly. Married by the Rev. Aaron Brown, Methodist. p 117

15 July 1797. Peter HAWTHORN and Mary Ann Oldham, 21. Sur. Charles Oldham. Wit. Kennon H. Dixon and William Hawthorn. Married 20 July by the Rev. Peter Wynne. p 103

21 March 1799. Peter HAWTHORNE and Ann Blackwell. Married by the Rev. Peter Wynne. Ministers' Returns p 370

23 September 1789. George HAY and Rebecca Broadnax. Richard Gregory consents. Sur. Thomas Carter. Wit. Frederick Broadnax and Eliza-beth Greogry. Married by the Rev. Thomas Lundie, Rector of St. Andrew's Parish. p 55

27 October 1795. Henry HAYES and Polly Clarke. Sur. Jones Williams.
Wit. George H. Jones. Married 4 November by the Rev. Aaron Brown,
Methodist. p 87

26 December 1791. Thomas HAYLEY and Nancy Vaughan. See Thomas Hailey.
Brunswick p 88

2 August 1794. John HAYMORE and Rebecca Maghee, of age. Sur. Mark
Haymore. Wit. N. Taylor and Cornelius Taylor. Married 14 August
by the Rev. John Loyd. p 81

20 December 1779. Britain Jones HAYMOUR and Susanna Avery, dau. of
John Avery who writes consent to Peter Pelham, Jr. Clerk of the
County. Sur. William Abernathy. p 23

22 April 1782. Thomas HAYNES and Frances Stith, dau. William Stith.
Sur. Joseph Mason. p 28

23 December 1797. John HEARN, Jr. and Nancy B. Linch, 21. Sur. William
Betty. Wit. James Brown, Betsey Linch and William Boswell.
Married 27 December by the Rev. Balaam Ezell, Baptist. p 102

28 October 1800. George HERMON and Nancy Bethshirse, dau. Ruth
Bethshirse. Sur. William Bethshirse. Married 5 November by the
Rev. Balaam Ezell, Baptist. p 123

- - 1787. John HESTENS and Nancy Ellice. Married by the Rev.
John King, Baptist. Ministers' Returns p 253

11 April 1808. Hamlin HICKS and Jean Powell. Sur. John R. Powell. p 166

22 April 1782. Capt. Isaac HICKS and Ann (Nancy) Booth, dau. Reuben
Booth, deceased, and Rebecca Booth. Sur. Binns Jones. Wit.
John Jones. p 28

26 November 1787. James HICKS and Judith Collier, dau. Charles Collier.
Sur. Isaac Hicks. Wit. Smith Collier. Married by the Rev. John
King, Baptist. p 47

Returned 4 February 1790. Jesse HICKS and Mary Callis Hudgins. Married
by the Rev. John King, Baptist. Ministers' Returns p 357

25 November 1771. John HICKS and Anne Harrison, dau. Benjamin Harrison.
Sur. Myhill Collier. Wit. Peter Pelham, Jr., Charles Collier,
James Hicks and John Ballard, Jr. p 10

24 January 1780. John HICKS and Rachel Williams. Sur. David Williams.
Writes own consent. p 24

18 September 1810. John HICKS and Nancy Bennett, 21. Sur. Richard
Hagood. p 176

22 April 1799. Jordan HICKS and Lucy Pettit, 21. Sur. Michael
Tarwater. p 112

27 April 1807. Paschal HICKS and Lucy Hall. Sur. James Harrison. Married 29 April by the Rev. Edward Dromgoole. p 161

24 December 1794. Thomas HICKS and Jean Hampton. Married by the Rev. Peter Wynne. Ministers' Returns p 363

24 January 1803. Gregory HIGHTOWER and Mary Trotter, ward of Richard Trotter. Sur. Isham R. Trotter. Married 10 February by the Rev. Peter Wynne. p 139

2 June 1773. Green HILL and Mary Seawell. Sur. Benjamin Seawell. Both of St. Andrew's Parish. p 13

24 February 1802. Herbert HILL and Nancy Dunn. Married by the Rev. Aaron Brown, Methodist. Ministers' Returns p 385

11 January 1781. Thomas HILL and Frances Smith, consent of Elizabeth Smith. Sur. Buckner Lanier. Wit. James Smith and John Smith. p 25

24 October 1758. William HILL and Priscilla Embry, widow. Sur. Thomas Stith. p 5

27 September 1790. William HILL and Sarah Lanier, dau. Ann Lanier. Sur. Miles Williams. Married 1 November by the Rev. Aaron Brown, Methodist. p 61

13 December 1777. William HINES and Elizabeth Turner, widow. Sur. David Hines. Wit. Sarah Hines. p 18

-    -   1787. Ussery HITCHCOCK and Molley Lunsford. Married by the Rev. John King, Baptist. Ministers' Returns p 253

8 March 1790. Frederick HOBBS and Sally Moss, dau. David Moss. Sur. Benjamin Jackson. Wit. Mark Jackson. Married by the Rev. John King, Baptist. p 59

-    -   1787. John HODGE and Jane Thornton. Married by the Rev. John King, Baptist. Ministers' Returns p 253

27 June 1797. Joseph HOLDERBY and Lucy Brander. Sur. John Jones. Married 6 July by the Rev. Hubbard Saunders. This name spelled several ways: Holobay. p 98

8 December 1787. Lewis HOLLOWAY and Rachel Williams. Sur. Roger Williams. Married by the Rev. Thomas Lundie, Rector of St. Andrew's Parish. p 47

23 December 1799. Silas HOLLOWAY and Abby Moseley, 21. Sur. Wyatt Edmunds. Wit. Radford Gunn. Married 25 December by the Rev. Balaam Ezell, Baptist. p 117

5 March 1791. Edward HOLMES and Hannah Mathews, over 21. Sur. William Mitchell. Wit. John Lett, William Stainback and John Jones. Married by the Rev. John Fore who says Edward Holmes of Mecklenburg County. p 64

13 December 1797. Isaac HOLMES and Frances Parham. A. Hill gives
consent. Sur. John C. Courtney. Wit. Hinchia Parham. Married
14 December by the Rev. John Loyd. p 101

15 June 1782. William HOLMES and Sarah Warren, widow of John Warren.
Sur. Sack Pennington. p 28

20 March 1797. James HOLSEY and Susanna Ingram. Sur. John Paup. Wit.
John Green. p 97

- July 1786. William HOLT and Frances Mabry. Married by the Rev.
Thomas Lundie, Rector of St. Andrew's Parish. Ministers'
Returns p 349

24 January 1800. Ambrose HOUSE and Polley Hartwell, 21. Sur. John
Owen. Married by the Rev. Ira Ellis. p 119

23 December 1799. Claiborne HOUSE and Polly Ledbetter, 21. Sur. Isaac
Ledbetter. Married 26 December by the Rev. Edward Dromgoole. p 117

25 October 1790. Drury HOUSE and Elizabeth Nash, 23. Sur. Robert
Harrison. Wit. Jonathan Doe and Richard Roe. Married by the
Rev. John King, Baptist. p 61

22 October 1804. Green HOUSE and Betsy Lanier. Sur. John Lanier. p 147

24 December 1798. Isaac Flood HOUSE and Elizabeth Neal, 21, dau. John
Neal, deceased. Susanna Neal makes affidavit as to her age. Sur.
John Neal. Wit. Enos Scarborough and Thomas Neal. Married by
the Rev. Balaam Ezell, Baptist. p 109

3 February 1810. Isaac HOUSE and Elizabeth Kelly, dau. Jesse Kelley.
Sur. Allen James. Married 6 February by the Rev. Cary James,
Methodist. p 174

21 February 1775. John HOUSE (or HOWSE) and Elizabeth Sims. Sur.
John Blanks. p 16

5 December 1803. John HOUSE and Kesiah Wesson. Sur. James Bass. p 143

21 December 1807. Joseph HOUSE and Sinthy Wray, dau. Reuben Wray. Sur.
Anderson James. Married by the Rev. Aaron Brown, Methodist who
says Cinthia Rhea. p 165

25 February 1771. Lawrence HOUSE and Lucy Hobbs. Sur. John Hobbs. p 9

- January 1788. Miles HOUSE and Sally Short. Married by the Rev.
John King, Baptist. Ministers' Returns p 253

22 January 1799. Phillip HOUSE and Nancy Collier, dau. Myhill Collier.
Married 24 January by the Rev. Balaam Ezell, Baptist. p 111

23 February 1784. Mordecai HOWARD and Jane Anderton, dau. Isaac
Anderton. Sur. John Jones. p 32

25 January 1791. Richard HOWARD and Elizabeth Anderton. Sur. John
Rose Williams. Wit. Mordecai Howard. Married 27 January by the
Rev. Aaron Brown, Methodist. p 64

22 December 1789. Thomas HOWARD and Betsey Ledbetter, dau. Jean Ledbetter. Sur. Mordecai Howard. Wit. George Johnston. Married by
the Rev. John King, Baptist. p 57

15 October 1808. Drury HOWERTON and Betsy Biggs. Sur. Richard Biggs.
Married 20 October by the Rev. Peter Wynne. p 168

24 March 1791. William HOWERTON and Martha Traylor, dau. Joseph Traylor.
Sur. Benjamin Roper. Wit. David Roper. Married by the Rev. Thomas
Lundie, Rector of St. Andrew's Parish. p 65

13 December 1796. Isham HOWSE and Betsey Gee, dau. Robert Gee. Sur.
Burwell Lanier. Wit. Baley Gee. Married 14 December by the Rev.
Peter Wynne. p 94

27 November 1786. John HUBBARD and Mary Gresham. Sur. Asa Gresham.
Married by the Rev. John King, Baptist. p 41

4 July 1802. Gregory HUDSON and Bridgett Davis, 21. Sur. Charles
Hagood, p 134

9 November 1793. James HUFF and Rebecca Moseley, dau. Samuel Moseley
who is surety. p 77

24 November 1793. Joseph HUFF and Keziah Cristie, 21. Sur. John
Phoenix. Wit. Ann Cristie and Sarah Burgess. p 77

24 December 1796. Julius HUFF and Huldah Moseley, dau. Samuel Moseley.
Sur. Phill Huff. Married 25 December by the Rev. Balaam Ezell,
Baptist. p 94

21 December 1796. Lundie HUFF and Pharaby Read, dau. Peter Read. Sur.
William Huff. Married by the Rev. Balaam Ezell, Baptist. p 93

3 August 1799. Lundy HUFF and Sarah White, dau. Blewmer White. Sur.
James Huff. Wit. John White. Married 8 August by the Rev. James
Meacham. p 114

27 April 1789. Thomas HUFF and Tabitha Huff, consent of Mary Huff.
Sur. James Huff. Wit. Daniel Huff. p 54

26 December 1769. Judkins HUNT and Martha Batte, ward of William
Batte. Sur. Robert Rivers. Wit. William Atkison. p 8

25 July 1758. Thomas HUNT and Atheliah Norris, widow, of St. Andrew's
Parish. Sur. Archibald Wager. Thomas Hunt of Sussex County.
p 4

31 January 1778. Turner HUNT and Ann Stainback, dau. of Francis Stainback. Sur. Thomas Rivers. Wit. Julius Perry. p 19

July 1788 - July 1789. William HUNT and Sarah Allgood. Married by the
Rev. John King, Baptist. Ministers' Returns p 354

15 October 1779. Charles HUTCHINS and Patty Green, widow. Sur. Edward
Jones. p 22

17 May 1797. Thomas B. HUTT and Elizabeth Bennett. Sur. John Bennett.
Married 18 May by the Rev. Hubbard Saunders. p 98

30 November 1803. Barthalomew INGRAM and Elizabeth Dunnington. Sur.
John Paup. Wit. Leonard W. Walker. p 143

20 December 1802. Benjamin INGRAM and Susanna Hardaway Manson, dau.
Thomas Manson. Sur. Paschal Jones. Wit. Sally Pegram. p 138

29 March 1802. Benjamin INGRAM and Sally Mason. Sur. R. Watson. p 166

26 March 1804. Henry INGRAM and Elizabeth Overby, 21. Sur. Jesse Westmoreland. Married 29 March by the Rev. Peter Wynne. p 146

22 November 1790. Thomas INGRAM and Mary Ann Ingram. Sur. Charles
Harris. Married by the Rev. Thomas Lundie, Rector of St. Andrew's
Parish. p 61

27 September 1802. Thomas INGRAM and Sally P. Hunnicut, 21. Sur.
Washington Croft. Wit. John Judd, Jr., and Henry Clay. Returned
10 November by the Rev. Peter Wynne. p 135

1 November 1769. Bedford IRWIN and Frances Jones. Sur. Mordecai Jones.
Wit. Francis Young and Elizabeth Steward. p 7

25 December 1807. James IVES and Celah Hill Lafoon. Married by the
Rev. Aaron Brown, Methodist. See James Ivey. Ministers' Returns
p 388

23 July 1806. Hardiman S. IVEY and Elizabeth Bass, dau. Partin and
Rebecca Bass. Sur. Anselem Ivey. Wit. Batts Tatum and Peter
Edwards. Married 30 July by the Rev. Hubbard Saunders. p 157

23 December 1807. James IVEY and Celah Hill Laffoon, 21. Sur. Henry
Russell. Brunswick say Celia. See James Ives. p 165

2 January 1799. Thomas IVEY and Catharine Connell, dau. William Connell.
Sur. Peter Ivey. Wit. Patty Connell. Married 6 January by the Rev.
Balaam Ezell, Baptist. p 110

28 May 1787. Benjamin IVY and Jane Woodrough, dau. George Woodrough.
Sur. Buckner Ezell. Married 8 June by the Rev. John King, Baptist.
p 44

8 February 1791. Allen JACKSON and Sally Scarbrough, over 21. Sur.
Jordan Jackson. Wit. Joseph Price and Daniel Duggar. Married
by the Rev. Aaron Brown, Methodist. p 64

20 November 1810. Burwell JACKSON and Nancy Baugh. Sur. Littleberry
Baugh. p 177

10 January 1809. Coleman JACKSON and Frances Richardson, dau. Jordan Richardson. Sur. William Mason. Married 12 January by the Rev. Edward Dromgoole. p 170

23 December 1793. David JACKSON and Martha Edwards, ward of John Hardaway. Sur. Washington Craft. Wit. Benjamin Smith and Ishmael Harwell. p 78

3 June 1798. David JACKSON and Polly Mason, 21. Benjamin Green makes affidavit as to her age. Sur. Herbert Hill. Wit. Henry Tatum, Paul Tatum, John Folkes and Robert Mitchell. p 105

21 December 1784. Henry JACKSON and Anne Broadnax, dau. Ann Broadnax. Sur. John Parish. p 34

5 September 1807. Green JACKSON and Rebecca R. Lucas, 21. Sur. Reubin B. Hicks. Wit. George H. Jones. Married by the Rev. Thomas Adams, Methodist. p 163

4 July 1797. Mark L. JACKSON and Leannah Basey Webb. Married by the Rev. Peter Wynne. Ministers' Returns p 366

27 February 1797. Randle JACKSON and Rebecca Britt. Benjamin Britt consents. Sur. Ephraim Jackson. Wit. Henry Britt. Married 7 March by the Rev. Edward Dromgoole. p 97

24 September 1759. Samuel JACKSON and Mary King, dau. Joseph King who is surety. p 6

27 September 1808. Stephen JACKSON and Jane Stainback. Sur. Green Hill. p 168

26 December 1808. William JACKSON and Susan Proch. Sur. John Phipps. p 169

4 May 1804. George JAMES and Jincy P. Powell, 21. Sur. David Kennedy consents only, see p. 151 for bond. p 146

4 May 1805. George JAMES and Jincy P. Powell, of age. Sur. David Kennedy. Wit. James Fisher. Married by the Rev. Peter Wynne. p 151

22 November 1802. John JAMES and Patsey Hancocke, of age, consent of Sarah Hancocke. Sur. Philip Claiborne. Married 9 December by the Rev. Ira Ellis. p 136

- - 1786. David JARROTT and Judy Mizes. Married by the Rev. John King, Baptist. Ministers' Returns p 349

11 March 1779. Thomas JENKINS and Elizabeth Major. Sur. Samuel Major, Jr. p 21

23 October 1786. Thomas JENKINS and Mary Washington, dau. Thomas Washington, deceased. Sur. Thomas Washington. Married by the Rev. Thomas Lundie, Rector of St. Andrew's Parish. p 41

8 September 1778. Andrew JETER and Mary Smith, consent of Eads Smith. Sur. Lewelling Williamson. p 20

4 January 1781. John JETER, Jr. and Elizabeth Tomlinson, widow. Sur. Edmund Jeter. p 25

13 October 1804. Capt Thomas JETT and Frances Starke, dau. Elizabeth Starke. Sur. William Stainback. Married by the Rev. Aaron Brown, Methodist. p 147

20 January 1807. Thornton JETT and Lucy Randolph, 21. Sur. Robert Jackson. Married by the Rev. Aaron Brown, Methodist. p 160

28 November 1808. Anderson JOHNSON and Catherine C. Greenhill. Sur. Green Hill. Married by the Rev. Thomas Adams, Methodist. p 168

26 May 1772. Benjamin JOHNSON and Isabella Chapman. Sur. Michael Wall. p 11

27 January 1786. Benjamin JOHNSON and Susanna Jackson, dau. Burwell Jackson. Sur. John Williams. Married by the Rev. Thomas Lundie, Rector of St. Andrew's Parish. p 38

16 May 1791. Charles JOHNSON and Patty Lightfoot, 21. Sur. William M. Johnson. Wit. Philip Lightfoot and Thomas Lightfoot. p 65

7 November 1796. David JOHNSON and Betsey L. Hammond. Sur. William Hammond. Returned 22 December by the Rev. John Rogers. p 92

19 July 1808. George JOHNSON and Elizabeth Croft. Sur. Miles Abernathy. p 167

14 September 1792. Henry JOHNSON and Milly Whealer, dau. Benjamin Whealer. Sur. Thomas Goodrum. Wit. Absalom Bennett. Married by the Rev. Edward Dromgoole. p 71

23 March 1789. James JOHNSON and Nancy Wright, dau. Sarah Wright. Sur. James Powell. Wit. Samuel Wright. Married by the Rev. John King, Baptist, who says Johnston. p 53

30 December 1789. James JOHNSON and Hannah Samford, 21. Sur. William Garner. Wit. John Lanier. p 57

15 April 1795. James Lucas JOHNSON and Nancy Allen. Sur. Robert Allen. Married 16 April by the Rev. Aaron Brown, Methodist. p 85

22 December 1806. Joel JOHNSON and Polly Goodrum, dau. Bennett Goodrum. Sur. William Johnson. Married 24 December by the Rev. Aaron Brown, Methodist. p 159

8 May 1801. Lewis JOHNSON and Lucretia Taylor, 21. Sur. Benjamin Phipps. Married 17 May by the Rev. Balaam Ezell, Baptist. p 127

23 November 1807. William JOHNSON and Nancy Miller. Sur. Benjamin
    Miller. Married 25 November by the Rev. Aaron Brown, Methodist.
    p 164

29 December 1807. William JOHNSON and Sally Johnson. Sur. Thomas
    Marks. Married by the Rev. Thomas Adams, Methodist. p 165

8 February 1809. William JOHNSON and Sarah Hood. Sur. Frederick Haw-
    thorn. Married 10 February by the Rev. Peter Wynne. p 170

28 July 1808. Claburn (Claibrone) JOLLY and Elizabeth Hoy. Married
    by the Rev. Peter Wynne. Ministers' Returns p 389

29 September 1798. Thomas JOLLY and Susanna Evans, 21. Sur. Francis
    Evans. Wit. John Evans. p 107

16 June 1807. Augustine C. JONES and Dionesia Ravenscroft Starke.
    Sur. Robert Turnbull. p 162

23 November 1801. Benjamin JONES and Dorothy Mabry. Sur. James
    Harrison. Wit. Sterling Ruffin. Married 25 November by the Rev.
    Aaron Brown, Methodist. p 129

25 February 1755. Berryman JONES and Lucretia Bryan. Sur. Thomas
    Bryan. p 2

1 September 1800. Christopher JONES and Martha Keatt, dau. James Keatt.
    Sur. Edward Jones Tarpley. Wit. Thomas Manson. p 122

16 July 1803. David JONES and Betsey Matthews, 21. Sur. Thomas
    Matthews. Wit. Luke Matthews. p 141

6 September 1793. Drury JONES and Mary Simmons, dau. Martha Field.
    Sur. Gale Lewis. Drury Jones of Dinwiddie County. p 77

11 January 1799. Francis JONES and Lucy Simmons, 21, dau. Martha Field.
    Sur. James Field and Edmund Field. p 110

1 November 1787. Frederick JONES and Nelly Brooks. Married by the
    Rev. John King, Baptist. Ministers' Returns p 253

27 January 1806. Frederick JONES and Sally Maclin. Sur. John Elliott.
    p 155

16 December 1786. Henry JONES and Sally Lightfoot. Sur. Thomas Light-
    foot. Married by the Rev. Thomas Lundie, Rector of St. Andrew's
    Parish. p 42

27 July 1801. Hicks JONES and Quintena Holloway. Sur. Asa Holloway.
    Married 1 August by the Rev. Balaam Ezell, Baptist. p 128

13 January 1778. Irwin JONES and Priscilla Dawson, dau. Samuel Dawson.
    Sur. Edward Jones. Wit. Daniel Mabry and John Jones. p 18

2 June 1787. John JONES, Jr. and Lucy Binns Cargill, ward of John
     Jones. Sur. Edmund Stith. Wit. Binns Jones and Charles B. Jones.
     Married by the Rev. Thomas Lundie, Rector of St. Andrew's Parish.
     p 45

17 May 1756. Joseph JONES and Ann Jones, widow. Sur. William Bishop.
     p 3

21 October 1803. Lamuel JONES and Betsy Weaver, 21. Sur. William
     Weaver. Married 22 October by the Rev. John Rogers. p 142

26 July 1807. Ned JONES and Dicey Lewis. Married by the Rev. Peter
     Wynne. Ministers' Returns p 384

19 January 1804. Reps. JONES and Frances Keatts, dau. Frances Keatts.
     Sur. Henry Keatts. Wit. Thomas Jones. p 145

26 January 1789. Samuel JONES and Elizabeth Butterill. Sur. Burwell
     Wilks. p 53

17 December 1804. Thomas JONES and Polly Burge. Sur. Bradford Burge.
     Returned 2 January 1805, by the Rev. Aaron Brown, Methodist. p 148

14 February 1792. William JONES and Agness Bolling Clack, 21. Wit.
     Richard Clack and Hinchia Mabry. William Jones of Greensville
     County. Sur. James Clack. p 69

31 March 1809. William JONES and Elizabeth Wesson, consent of Isaac
     Wesson. Wit. Washington Wesson. Married 6 April by the Rev. Cary
     James, Methodist. p 171

24 October 1781. Arthur JORDAN and Elizabeth Williams, widow. Sur.
     George King. Arthur Jordan of North Carolina. p 26

21 April 1778. John JORDAN and Mary Winfield. Sur. Edward Winfield.
     p 19

15 December 1804. John JUDD and Frances R. Cousins, of age. Sur.
     Thomas Judd. Married 20 December by the Rev. Peter Wynne. p 148

16 December 1802. Thomas JUDD and Mary Kelly, dau. Samuel Kelly. Sur.
     John Judd. Wit. James Kelly, Jr. and David Kelly. Married
     23 December by the Rev. Peter Wynne. p 137

8 February 1809. Daniel JUSTICE and Tabitha Ogborne. Sur. William
     Morgain. p 170

7 May 1793. Mark JUSTICE and Mary Wesson, 21. Sur. William Wesson.
     Wit. Henry Kelly and David Kelly. Married 14 May by the Rev.
     Edward Dromgoole. p 75

27 July 1795. Mark JUSTICE and Nelly Wray. Sur. John Wray. Married
     10 August by the Rev. Aaron Brown, Methodist. p 86

29 August 1798. William JUSTICE and Rahab Edmunds, of age. Sur. Plea-
     sant Smith. Wit. John Wesson and Isaac Wesson. Married by the
     Rev. Balaam Ezell, Baptist. p 106

12 October 1797. William KASH (Cash?) and Elizabeth Brown. Married by the Rev. Peter Wynne. Ministers' Returns p 368

11 November 1799. Henry KEATTS and Betsey Moss, 21, dau. David Moss. Sur. Meredith Moss. Wit. David Moss and Sally Hobbs. p 115

19 November 1795. Lewis KELLEY and Alice Abernathy. Sur. William Abernathy. Married by the Rev. Aaron Brown, Methodist. p 87

24 July 1805. Thomas KELLEY and Lucy Stith, dau. Thomas Stith. Sur. Gideon Purkins. Wit. Lewis Kelley. Married 7 August by the Rev. Aaron Brown, Methodist. p 151

4 January 1781. Giles KELLY and Jane Constable. Sur. Garner Scoggin. p 25

26 April 1802. James KELLY, Jr. and Angeline Overby, 21. Sur. David Kelly. Wit. Edmund Kelly. Married 5 May by the Rev. Peter Wynne who says Angelica. p 133

5 January 1787. Jesse KELLY and Patty Phillips, dau. Elizabeth Phillips. Sur. Isaac Wesson. Wit. Benjamin Seward. p 43

19 November 1807. Lewis KELLY and Sarah B. Wilson, dau. John Wilson, Sr. Sur. Thomas Overby. Wit. John Wilson, Jr. p 164

23 January 1797. William KELLY and Nancy S. Penn. Married 26 January by the Rev. Aaron Brown, Methodist. Brunswick p 106

24 April 1809. Jesse KENNADY and Susanna Manson. Sur. John Manson. Married 29 April by the Rev. Peter Wynne. p 171

3 June 1806. William KENNADY and Earman Browder, dau. Susanna Browder. Sur. James Barnes. Wit. William Johnson. Married 7 June by the Rev. Aaron Brown, Methodist. p 156

5 April 1786. William H. KENNEDY and Betsy Pilkington. See William Cannady. Brunswick. p 106

14 December 1791. William KENNEDY and Rebecca Jordan. See William Canady. Brunswick p 106

30 March 1784. Thomas KERBY and Nancy Mallory, dau. Richard Mallory who is surety. See Thomas Kirby. p 33

26 June 1809. Joseph KIDD and Sally Pennington. Sur. Edwin Clarke. p 172

30 January 1778. Charles KING and Mary Celey, dau. William Celey. Sur. Merritt Celey. Wit. Cuddy Harrison. Double wedding: see Marritt Celey which gives a suggestion as to the father of Charles King. p 19

24 August 1783. Edward KING and Winefred Ledbetter, dau. Henry Ledbetter. Sur. George King. Wit. John Allen. p 31

17 December 1787. Edward KING and Patty Short, dau. John Short who is surety. Married by the Rev. Thomas Lundie, Rector of St. Andrew's Parish. p 48

20 October 1787. John W. KING and Susanna Short, dau. Armistead Short. Brunswick p 108

23 January 1802. John KING and Obedience Turpin Parham, dau. William Parham. Sur. Richard Evans. Wit. George Melor. p 132

21 March 1785. Lewis KING and Becke Birdsong, dau. James Birdsong. Sur. Freeman Birdsong. p 35

22 August 1808. Miles KING and Martha Short, dau. John C. Short who is surety. p 167

22 December 1794. William KING and Betsey Moore, dau. William Moore who is surety. p 83

22 January 1795. William KING and Elizabeth Moore. Married by the Rev. Peter Wynne. Ministers' Returns p 363

24 November 1798. William KING and Susannah J. Elder. Married by the Rev. Peter Wynne. Ministers' Returns p 370

30 March 1784. Thomas KIRBY and Nancy Mallory, dau. Roger Mallory. See Thomas Kerby. Brunswick p 108

8 April 1804. David KIRKLAND and Nancy Flax. Married by the Rev. Hubbard Saunders. Ministers' Returns p 381

10 September 1799. John KIRKLAND and Brambley Edwards, dau. Jesse Edwards. Sur. James Harwell. Married 12 September by the Rev. Aaron Brown, Methodist. p 114

10 May 1806. Richard KIRKLAND and Polly Granger, ward of Samuel Ingram. Sur. Rucker Kirkland. Wit. John Turner, Jr., and Arealius Walker. Married by the Rev. Hubbard Saunders. p 156

Returned 4 February 1790. William KIRKS and Jane Arnold. Married by the Rev. John King, Baptist. Ministers' Returns p 357

- - 1789. Thomas LADD and Polly Crowder. Married by the Rev. John King, Baptist. Ministers' Returns p 354

11 January 1803. Daniel LAFFOON and Caty Russell. Sur. Isaac Russell. Married 13 January by the Rev. Aaron Brown, Methodist. p 139

23 November 1789. James LAFFOON and Jincey Samford. Sur. Matthew Laffoon. Married by the Rev. Thomas Lundie, Rector of St. Andrew's Parish, who says Jeany. p 56

26 May 1800/ James LAFFOON and Elizabeth R. Burks, 21. Sur. Simon Laffoon. Wit. Weatherinton Preston. Married 29 May by the Rev. John Neblett. p 121

12 December 1803. Simon LAFFON and Milly Wiltshire, 21. Sur. Benjamin Moore. p 143

3 April 1804. John LAMBAND and Rebecca Reese. Married by the Rev. Peter Wynne. Ministers' Returns p 380

11 June 1795. Jeremiah LAMBERT and Sarah Cordle. Sur. Laban Petillo. p 86

4 September 1792. Lewis LAMBERT and Mildred Petillo, 21. Mary Petillo makes affidavit as to her age. Sur. Laban Pittillo. Wit. David Petillo. Married by the Rev. John Paup. p 71

3 June 1797. Lewis LAMBERT and Mary Waller. Married by the Rev. Peter Wynne. Ministers' Returns p 366

20 April 1780. John LANGTON and Sarah Ann Harrison. Sur. Henry Bishop. p 24

25 November 1771. Benjamin LANIER and Elizabeth Parker. Sur. Hinchey Pettway. p 10

10 November 1782. Benjamin LANIER and Ann Wilkerson. Married by Rev. John King, Baptist. Returned 17 January 1783. Ministers' Returns p 345

27 August 1804. Benjamin LANIER and Susan Hunnicut. Sur. Benjamin Hunnicut. Married 6 September by the Rev. Wright Tucker, Episcopal Rector. p 147

13 March 1794. Bird LANIER and Sarah Oast, of age. Sur. John Bulkley. Wit. Littleton Sims and John Bulkley, Jr. Married by the Rev. Aaron Brown, Methodist. p 80

22 August 1794. Burwell LANIER and Elizabeth Pepper. Sur. Elisha Riddle. Wit. Nathan Pepper and William Pepper. p 82

13 October 1805. Burwell LANIER and Elizabeth McKenny. Sur. James McKenny. p 152

26 December 1791. Collier LANIER and Lucy Berryman. Sur. Jesse Berryman. Married 29 December by the Rev. Aaron Brown, Methodist. p 68

24 November 1789. David LANIER and Frances Harwell, 21. Mary Lanier makes affidavit as to her age. Sur. Charles Harrison. Wit. Cuddy Harrison. Married by the Rev. Thomas Lundie, Rector of St. Andrew's Parish. p 56

5 May 1774. Drury LANIER and Tabitha Eves. Sur. Joseph Peebles. p 15

26 August 1793. Edmund LANIER and Patsey Walton. Sur. George Walton. Wit. John Wray and Braxton Wray. Married 29 August by the Rev. Edward Dromgoole. p 76

4 April 1807. Francis LANIER and Mary Branch Parham, 21. Sur.
William Avery. Married 5 April by the Rev. William Dossey,
Baptist. p 161

July 1787 - July 1788. Frederick LANIER and Elizabeth Williamson.
Married by the Rev. Thomas Lundie, Rector of St. Andrew's Parish.
Ministers' Returns p 352

23 January 1797. Frederick LANIER and Temperance Warren. Sur. Herbert
Hill. Wit. James Bass and Hartwell Bass. Married by the Rev.
Hubbard Saunders. p 95

25 November 1805. Henry LANIER and Martha Owen, dau. Robert Owen.
Sur. Edmund Short. p 153

17 July 1789. John LANIER and Selah Saunders, dau. Edward Saunders,
deceased; ward of Ebbin Saunders. Sur. James Penticost. Married
by the Rev. Thomas Lundie, Rector of St. Andrew's Parish who says
Cely. p 55

15 November 1806. John LANIER and Polly Wilson, dau. John Wilson. This
is an error; original bond says John Lenoir. See John Lenior.
Brunswick p 110

25 November 1752. Lewis LANIER and Martha Speed. Sur. James Speed.
p 1

12 December 1787. Nicholas LANIER and Patsey Malone, dau. George Malone.
Sur. Miles Malone. Wit. Allan Lanier. Married by the Rev. John
King, Baptist. p 48

9 September 1759. Robert LANIER and - Jackson, dau. John Jackson.
Sur. Peter Jackson. Wit. Daniel Jackson. p 6

24 November 1800. Robert LANIER and Nancy Harrison. Sur. Herbert Hill.
p 123

16 October 1792. Sterling LANIER and Hummons Westmoreland, consent of
Reaves and Susanna Westmoreland. Sur. Arhtur Fort. Wit. Nathaniel
Edwards and Benjamin Smith. p 72

23 February 1803. Sterling LANIER and Polly Avery, 21. Sur. James C.
Edwards. Married 24 February by the Rev. Peter Wynne. p 140

22 August 1794. Thomas LANIER and Polly Vaughan. Sur. Thomas Vaughan.
p 82

4 April 1807. Thomas LANIER and Mary B. Parham. This is an error; the
original bond says Francis Lanier. See Francis Lanier. Brunswick
p 112

7 November 1809. Thomas LANIER and Mary Peebles, dau. Jesse Peebles.
Sur. Edmund Short. Wit. Nicholas Lanier. p 172

5 November 1810. Thomas LANIER, Jr. and Martha Dunkley. Sur. Nicholas
Lanier. Wit. Abner Wesson and David Crooks. p 177

23 August 1779. Benjamin LASHLEY and Martha Harrison. Sur. William Harrison. p 22

23 September 1771. John LASHLEY and Rebecca Flether, under age, dau. of John Fletcher. Sur. Owen Myril. p 10

5 February 1801. William LASHLEY and Naomy Harrison. Sur. Robert Harrison. Married 11 February by the Rev. James Meacham. p 126

26 December 1791. Robert LATIMER and Martha Talley. Sur. Jesse Penn. Wit. David Petillo. Married by the Rev. Thomas Lundie, Rector of St. Andrew's Parish. p 68

11 February 1797. William LATIMER and Rebecca Elder. Married by the Rev. Peter Wynne. Ministers' Returns p 366

29 April 1788. John LATTIMORE and Betsey Wilson. Sur. John Wilson. Married by the Rev. Thomas Lundie, Rector of St. Andrew's Parish. p 50

21 September 1803. John LEACH and Susan Parham. Sur. Thomas Parham. Married 22 December by the Rev. Hubbard Saunders. p 142

22 October 1804. Hamlin LEADBETTER and Dicey Wright. Sur. John Wright. Married 2 November by the Rev. Edward Dromgoole. p 147

26 December 1808. Hubbard LEDBETTER and Thirzor Moseley. Sur. Sion Linch. Returned 16 February 1809, by the Rev. Edward Dromgoole who says Thirza. p 169

22 December 1797. Isaac LEDBETTER and Nancy King, 21. Sur. William Carpenter. Wit. Benjamin King and John King. Married 24 December by the Rev. Edward Dromgoole. p 102

7 December 1809. Osborne LEDBETTER and Polly Delbridge. See Ogburn Ledbetter. Brunswick p 112

7 December 1809. Ozburn LEDBETTER and Polly Delbridge, 21. Sur. Washington Wesson. Married 14 December by the Rev. Cary James, Methodist. See Osborne Ledbetter. p 173

19 December 1801. David LEE and Fanny Moore. Sur. William Morre. Married 24 December by the Rev. Peter Wynne. p 131

- April 1786. James LEE and Mary Collier. Married by the Rev. Thomas Lundie, Rector of St. Andrew's Parish. Ministers' Returns p 348

22 December 1810. James LEE and Clerky Kelly, of age. Sur. Thomas Judd. Wit. Joshua Lucy. Married 27 December by the Rev. Peter Wynne. p 178

19 June 1806. Wyatt LEE and Dolly Grant. Married by the Rev. Peter Wynne. Ministers' Returns p 382

15 November 1806. John LENOIR and Polly Wilson, consent of John
Wilson. Sur. John Cheely. Wit. James Quarles. Married 19 November by the Rev. Peter Wynne. See John Lanier. p 158

14 March 1780. James LETT and Lucy Hubbard. Sur. Thomas Grubbs.
Wit. Littleberry Avery. p 24

24 November 1777. John LETT and Jean Winfield. Sur. Benjamin Walker.
Wit. Luke Mathis. p 18

6 February 1801. John LETT and Elizabeth Walker, of age. Sur. Herbert
Hill. Wit. Hinson Harrison and Patsy Hall. Married by the Rev.
James Meacham. p 126

27 December 1794. William LETT and Polly Duggar, dau. John Duggar.
Sur. Lewis Bennett. Wit. John Freeman and Thomas Edmunds.
Returned 22 January 1794 by the Rev. Aaron Brown, Methodist. p 83

18 March 1770. Thomas LEWELLING and Sarah Adams. Sur. Seymour Powell.
p 8

8 September 1787. Benjamin LEWIS and Elizabeth Edmunds, dau. John Flood
Edmunds. Sur. Griffin Stith. Married by the Rev. Thomas Lundie,
Rector of St. Andrew's Parish. p 46

25 June 1787. Harbert LEWIS and Charlotte Betty, dau. Thomas and Genny
Betty. Sur. Growner Owen. p 45

28 January 1793. John LEWIS and Lucy Maclin, 21. Frederick Maclin makes
affidavit as to her age. Sur. Thomas Maclin. Wit. Herbert Hill.
p 74

7 August 1787. Reuel LEWIS and Silvy Abernathy, dau. Frederick Abernathy who is surety. p 45

27 November 1786. Claiborne LIGHTFOOT and Betsey Wray, dau. John Wray
who is surety. p 41

4 January 1803. Nathaniel LILLEY and Judith King, dau. Charles King, Sr.
Sur. John Powell. Married 5 January by the Rev. Ira Ellis. p 139

17 April 1800. Adin LINCH and Sally Jones, 21. Sur. Uriah Brock. p 120

27 June 1803. Lewis LINCH and Amey Moseley. Sur. Samuel Moseley. p 141

25 January 1802. Syrick LINCH and Sally Mosley. Sur. Samuel Moseley.
p 132

25 October 1802. William LINCH and Nancy Wright, dau. John Wright.
Sur. Asa Holloway. Wit. Sion Lynch and James Linch. Married
2 November by the Rev. Edward Dromgoole. p 136

16 October 1787. William LLOYD and Lucy Scarbrough, dau. William Scarbrough. Sur. Moses Pritchett. Married by the Rev. Thomas Lundie,
Rector of St. Andrew's Parish. p 46

19 December 1797. William LLOYD and Polly Thrift. Sur. Joseph Samford. Wit. William Scarbrough. Married by the Rev. Aaron Brown, Methodist. p 101

15 December 1809. Philip LOCKETT and Jane Trotter. Sur. James Trotter. p 173

5 November 1798. Allan LOVE and Mary Edmunds, dau. Sterling Edmunds. Sur. Herbert Hill. p 107

5 November 1793. Edward LOVE and Lucy Harrison, 21. Sur. Theophilus Harrison. Wit. James H. Harrison. Married 7 November by the Rev. Daniel Southall. p 77

4 April 1771. Hugh LOVE and Elizabeth Huling Thomas, granddau. of Edward Hewlin. Sur. Francis Young. Wit. Nathan Hall. p 9

22 March 1798. John LOVE and Frances Harrison, 21. Sur. James H. Harrison. Wit. Theo. Harrison. Married 23 March by the Rev. James Meacham. p 104

13 December 1798. Robert LOVE and Mary Shelburne. Married by the Rev. Peter Wynne. Ministers' Returns p 370

12 December 1796. Henry LOYD and Sally Petillo, 21. Sur. Lewis Brown. Wit. Robert Harrison and Edward Edwards. Married 15 December by the Rev. Aaron Brown, Methodist. p 93

6 August 1803. Stephen LOYD and Elizabeth Johnson. Sur. William M. Johnson. Married 10 August by the Rev. Aaron Brown, Methodist. p 141

9 January 1797. Frederick LUCY and Ann Burge, dau. Nathaniel Burge. Sur. William Kelly. Wit. Joshua Lucy. Married 12 January by the Rev. Aaron Brown, Methodist. p 95

18 December 1792. Isham LUCY and Elizabeth Johnson, dau. William Johnson. Sur. David Meredith. Married 20 December by the Rev. Aaron Brown, Methodist. p 72

27 February 1797. Jesse LUCY and Betsey Westmoreland. Sur. Washington Croft. p 97

18 September 1787. Joshua LUCY and Elizabeth Kelly, dau. Samuel Kelly. Sur. Thomas Ingram. p 46

4 November 1794. Robert LUCY and Mary Kelly Browder, dau. Joseph Browder. Sur. James Barnes. Wit. Thomas Fowlkes. Married 6 November by the Rev. Aaron Brown, Methodist. p 82

21 October 1799. Robert LUCY and Catharine Abernathy. Sur. Frederick Abernathy. Married 22 October by the Rev. Hubbard Saunders. p 114

18 June 1800. Thomas Y. LUNDIE and Elizabeth Maclin. Married by the Rev. Aaron Brown, Methodist. Ministers' Returns p 374

29 October 1778. William LUNDIE and Lydia Garriss, dau. Hannah Garriss; ward of John Sturgeon. Sur. John Brett. Wit. Celia Sturgeon and John Brett. p 20

15 April 1809. Joseph LUNDSFORD and Susanna Pitman. Married by the Rev. Peter Wynne. Ministers' Returns p 389

24 December 1753. Thomas LYALL and Rebecca Tatum. Sur. Peter Tatum. p 2

4 March 1801. James M -   , Jr. and Elizabeth Jones. Married by the Rev. Aaron Brown, Methodist. Ministers' Returns p 377

15 January 1794. Gray MABRY and Martha Watson, dau. William Watson. Sur. Robert Watson. Wit. William Watson, Jr. p 79

28 May 1787. Hinchia MABRY and Dolly Clack, dau. John Clack, deceased and Mary Clack. Sur. James Clack. Wit. Elizabeth Clack. Married by the Rev. Thomas Lundie, Rector of St. Andrew's Parish. p 45

10 September 1770. Jordan MABRY and Ann Harwell, dau. James Harwell. Mordan Mabry of Macklenburg County, son of Joshua Mabry. Sur. John Clack. Wit. Joshua Mabry and Morning Harwell. p 9

10 September 1770. Joshua MABRY and -   -. Brunswick p 116

16 February 1773. Lewis MABRY and Susanna Hamilton. Sur. Joel Mabry. Wit. John Hamilton and William Hamilton. p 13

2 April 1779. Robert MABRY and Rebecca Stewart. Robert son of Nathaniel Mabry who is surety. p 22

July 1787 - July 1788. Robert MABRY and Rebecca Mason. Married by the Rev. Thomas Lundie, Rector of St. Andrew's Parish. Ministers' Returns p 351

16 June 1772. Seth MABRY and Elizabeth Seawell, consent of Joel Mabry. Sur. Benjamin Seawell, Sr. Wit. Joel Wilkinson, Benjamin Mathews, Peter Pelham, Jr., Isaac Collier. p 11

14 November 1799. Augustin W. MACLIN and Polly Jones. Sur. Herbert Hill. p 115

11 November 1782. James MACLIN and Lucy Jones. Wm. & M. Q. 1st. Ser. Vol. VII p 38: July 1898

29 March 1773. Col. John MACLIN and Ann Cryer, widow. Sur. Joseph Peebles. p 13

17 February 1806. John D. MACLIN and Charlotte Edmunds, consent of Thomas Edmunds. Sur. Edwin Edmunds. Married by the Rev. Aaron Brown, Methodist. p 155

14 March 1796. Joseph MACLIN and Nancy Walker, dau. David Walker. Wm. & M. Q. 1st Ser. Vol. VII p 38: July 1898

14 July 1800. Thomas MACLIN and Julis Edmunds, dau. Lucy Edmunds.
Sur. James Edmunds. Wit. Abner Wesson. Married 17 July by the
Rev. Aaron Brown, Methodist. p 122

25 September 1754. William MACLIN, Jr. and Sally Clack, dau. James
Clack. Va. Mag. Vol. XXVIII p 168; April 1920. Wm. & M.Q. 1st Sev.
Vol. VII p 37: July 1898.

25 September 1786. Lazarus MADDUX and Hannah Jones, widow of John R.
Jones. Sur. John Green. Married by the Rev. Thomas Lundie, Rector
of St. Andrew's Parish who says Anne Jones. p 40

29 September 1781. Wilfred MADDOX and Lucretia Bishop, dau. Matthew
Bishop. Sur. William Bishop. p 26

6 November 1805. Israel MAIRS and Lucy Serivant (?) (Sturdivant?).
Sur. James H. Hardaway. See Isarel Morris. p 152

25 September 1797. Richard MAITLAND and Sally Dugger. Sur. John
Dugger, Jr. Married by the Rev. Aaron Brown, Methodist. p 100

3 January 1807. Samuel MAJOR and Elizabeth Green, dau. Dorothy Green.
Sur. Charles Oldham. p 160

24 October 1788. Robert MALLORY, Jr. and Tabitha Baugh. Sarah Baugh,
guardian. Sur. Richard Clack. Married by the Rev. Thomas Lundie,
Rector of St. Andrew's Parish. p 51

24 May 1786. William MALLORY and Sarah Atkins, dau. John Atkins.
Sur. Zachariah Sims. p 39

27 January 1777. George MALONE and Lucy Carter. Sur. James Marshall.
p 17

9 May 1807. James MALONE and Martha Davis, dau. John Davis and ward
of James Batte. Sur. Jordan Malone. Wit. Polly Jackson and
Binns Jackson. James Malone "21 on the 17 March last", son
George Malone. p 161

24 November 1806. John P. MALONE and Sally Hobbs, dau. Hubbard Hobbs.
Sur. Green Hill. Wit. Ira Ellis. p 159

21 October 1776. Michael MALONE and Cicily Pettway, dau. Elizabeth
Pettway. Sur. Michael Malone. p 17

23 January 1786. Joel MANNING and Mary Owen, dau. William Owen who is
surety. Married 26 January by the Rev. John King, Baptist. p 36

27 July 1807. Thomas MANNING and Sally Seward. Sur. William Manning.
p 162

24 March 1794. William MANNING and Nancy Manning. Sur. Caleb Manning.
Married 27 March by the Rev. Edward Dromgoole. p 80

27 September 1802. William MANNING and Elizabeth Seward. Sur. James Nolley. p 135

25 January 1790. John MANSON and Elizabeth Rogers, dau. John Rogers. Sur. Thomas Manson. Wit. George Rogers. p 58

9 December 1803. Samuel MARKS and Martha L. Morris. Sur. Lester Morris. Married by the Rev. Aaron Brown, Methodist. p 143

10 December 1798. Thomas MARKS and Martha Brown, dau. Lewis Brown, Sr. Sur. Lester Morris. Married 13 December by the Rev. Aaron Brown, Methodist. p 108

30 July 1799. Benjamin MARRABLE and Lucy Barner, dau. John Barner. Sur. Stephen White. Married 21 August by the Rev. James Meacham. p 113

22 September 1795. Icabod MARSHALL and Sarah Harwell. Sur. Buckner Harwell. p 86

5 January 1789. James MARSHALL and Mary Williams. Sur. Lewis Williams. p 53

5 August 1799. John MARSHALL and Betty Jones Wynne. Sur. Peter Wynne. Married 8 August by the Rev. Peter Wynne. p 114

10 October 1796. Spain MARSHALL and Unity Johnson, of age. Sur. Edmund Collier. Wit. B. H. Hicks. Married 17 November (?) by the Rev. Balaam Ezell, Baptist. p 91

Returned 4 February 1790. Epps MARYMAN and Amey Kirks. Married by the Rev. John King, Baptist. Ministers' Returns p 357

23 May 1808. James MASON and Polly Hancocke, 21. Sur. Francis Hancock. p 167

4 February 1790. John MASON and Elizabeth Rogers. Married by the Rev. John Rogers. Ministers' Returns p 355

9 February 1799. John R. MASON and Sarah H. Cargill. Sur. John Jones. p 111

4 March 1783. Joseph MASON and Elizabeth Watson, dau. William Watson. Sur. Edmund Webb. Wit. John Mason. p 30

14 December 1807. Nathaniel MASON and Nancy Trotter. Sur. William Trotter. Married 16 December by the Rev. Aaron Brown, Methodist. p 165

10 November 1806. John MASSENBURG, Jr. and Sarah C. Jones. Sur. John C. Jones. Wit. George H. Jones. Married 13 November by the Rev. Edward Dromgoole. p 158

26 December 1810. William MASSEY and Margaret Kelly. Sur. Benjamin Justice. Married 27 December by the Rev. Cary James, Methodist. p 178

10 December 1788. James MATTHEWS and Elizabeth Hardie, consent of
Richard Hardy. Sur. Abraham Cocke. p 51

3 December 1790. John MATHEWS and Nancy Quarles, dau. Moses Quarles.
Sur. Vines Mathis. Wit. Frederick Briggs and Lewid Reed. Married
by the Rev. Thomas Lundie, Rector of St. Andrew's Parish who says
John Mathis. p 62

July 1788 - July 1789. Luke MATHEWS and Rebecca Dameron. Married by
the Rev. Thomas Lundie, Rector of St. Andrew's Parish. Ministers'
Returns p 254

6 May 1803. Robert MATHEWS and Jinsey Jones. Married by the Rev.
Peter Wynne. Ministers' Returns p 381

11 June 1792. Sugar Jones MATHIS and Angelica Jones Mathis, dau. Drury
Mathis. Sur. William Elmore. Wit. Charles Haskins and Eliza
Haskins. Married by the Rev. John Paup. p 70

19 December 1802. Drury MATTHEWS and Polley Wynne, 21. Sur. Jeremiah
Matthews. p 138

25 December 1794. John MATTHEWS and Frances Miskell. Married by the
Rev. Peter Wynne. Ministers' Returns p 363

25 December 1809. Luke MATTHEWS and Hannah H. Jones, dau. Samuel Jones.
Sur. Samuel H. Jones. Wit. James Fisher, Sr. Married by the Rev.
Peter Wynne. p 173

26 April 1802. Samuel MATTHEWS and Susanne Eppes. Sur. Richard Eppes.
Married 29 April by the Rev. Peter Wynne. p 133

26 August 1788. Wines MATTHEWS and Anne Morehead Dameron. Sur. Charles
Dameron. Wit. John Connally and John Matthews. Vines Mathews son
of Drury Matthews. p 50

26 October 1807. William MATTHEWS and Rebecca Taylor. Sur. Thomas
Taylor. Married 30 October by the Rev. Aaron Brown, Methodist.
p 163

26 May 1780. John MATTHIS and Rebecca Lawrence. Sur. John Lawrence.
p 24

21 December 1796. Matthew MATTHIS and Elizabeth Floyd, 21, dau. Ann
Floyd. Sur. Morris Floyd. Wit. Drury Quarles. p 94

18 October 1808. John Fitzhugh MAY and Margaret B. Field. Sur. Thomas
Simmons. John F. May of Petersburg, Dinwiddie County. Married
19 October by the Rev. Wright Tucker, Episcopal Rector. p 168

19 December 1785. William MAYS and Rebecca Morris, of age. Sur. Lester
Morris. Of St. Andrew's Parish. Married by the Rev. Thomas Lundie.
p 36

5 June 1797. James MEACHAM and Polly Seward. Sur. John Seward. p 98

5 December 1809. Jesse MEACHAM and Polly Birchett, dau. Nanney (illegible) mother. Sur. Lewis Barrow. Married 21 December by the Rev. Peter Wynne. p 173

18 September 1772. Andrew MEADE and Susanna Stith, dau. Buckner Sith. Andrew of Nansemond County and brother of David Meade of Nansemond County. Sur. Francis Young. Wit John Stith. p 11

23 July 1804. George MEALER and Olive Harrison, dau. Cuddy Harrison. Sur. Willie Short. Married 9 February by the Rev. Wright Tucker, Episcopal Rector. p 145

24 July 1808. James MEANLY and Mary Meanly, ward of Thomas Hamlin. Sur. James Pritchett. Married 27 July by the Rev. Peter Wynne. p 167

11 December 1793. Richard MEANLY and Elizabeth Traylor, 21. Sur. Edward Traylor. Wit. Lucy Traylor. p 78

1 March 1803. Richard MELONE and Martha Meanley. Married by the Rev. Peter Wynne. Ministers' Returns p 381

20 January 1782. David MEREDITH, Jr. and Elizabeth Winfield, dau. Joshua Winfield. Sur. Drury Stith. Wit. Freeman Winfield and Hubbard Hobbs. p 28

27 September 1807. David MEREDITH, Jr. and Mary W. Mason. Sur. Robert Watson. Married 30 September by the Rev. Aaron Brown, Methodist. p 163

24 November 1801. William MEREDITH and Writter Hamlett. Sur. Herbert Hill. p 129

24 December 1804. Charles MERRETT and Fortune Jackson. Sur. John Wyche. Wit. Peter Wyche and John Roberts. p 149

22 December 1800. Jacob MILLER and Nancy Brown, Sur. Aaron Brown. Wit. John Wyche. Returned 8 January 1801 by the Rev. John Neblett. p 125

17 December 1801. Anselm MINOR and Patsy Cook, 21. Sur. Ezekiel Blanch. Wit. Milly Cook and John Cook. Married 24 December by the Rev. James Meacham. p 131

18 October 1786. Peter MINER and Hannah Jones, dau. Peter Jones who is surety. Peter Minor of Dinwiddie County. Married by the Rev. Thomas Lundie, Rector of St. Andrew's Parish. p 41

11 October 1785. Thomas MINER and Tabitha Williams. Sur. William Williams. p 36

16 November 1804. William MINGE and Lucy Davis. Ministers' Returns p 380

- October 1785. Thomas MINOR and Elizabeth Williams. Married by the Rev. Thomas Lundie, Rector of St. Andrew's Parish. Ministers' Returns p 345

2 August 1796. Abram MITCHELL and Rebecca Hawthorn. Sur. Peter Hawthorn. Married 4 August by the Rev. Peter Wynne who says Abraham. p 91

17 December 1795. Benjamin MITCHELL and Mary Stone. Married by the Rev. Aaron Brown, Methodist. Ministers' Returns p 365

20 December 1806. Jesse MITCHELL and Patsey Adkins, 21. Sur. William Adkins. Married 22 December by the Rev. Peter Wynne who says Martha. p 159

10 September 1798. Joshua MITCHELL and Prudence Phillips, consent of Thomas Phillips. Sur. David Elam. Wit. Alexander Warwick. Married 26 September by the Rev. Aaron Brown, Methodist. p 106

15 February 1803. Marcus MITCHELL and Elizabeth Parham, 21. Sur. Thomas Orgain. Married 17 February by the Rev. Aaron Brown, Methodist. p 140

13 January 1803. Robert MITCHELL and Polley Collier. Sur. Nathaniel Collier. Married by the Rev. Aaron Brown, Methodist. p 139

26 October 1807. Thomas MITCHELL and Ann Moore. Sur. Cuddy Cheely. Wit. Ann Mitchell and Thomas Mitchell. Married 3 November by the Rev. Peter Wynne. p 164

13 January 1759. William MITCHELL and Mary Spears, dau. William and Ann Spears. Sur. Alexander Pool. (consent only)? p 5

27 June 1801. Dennis MIZE and Amey Ray, of age. Sur. Sterling Parker. Wit. Balaam Ezell. Married 8 July by the Rev. Balaam Ezell, Baptist. p 127

2 January 1794. Henry MIZE and Keziah Overby, 21. Sur. Cheslin Curtis. Married 11 January by the Rev. John Loyd. p 79

24 January 1791. Jeremiah MIZE, Jr. and Martha Mize. Sur. Jeremiah Mize, Sr. Wit. Herbert Hill. Married by the Rev. John King, Baptist. p 63

30 -   1786. Joseph MOON and Jane Johnson. Married by the Rev. John King, Baptist. Ministers' Returns p 349

11 January 1791. Benjamin MOORE and Elizabeth Laffoon, of age. Sur. Matthew Laffoon. Married 13 January by the Rev. Aaron Brown, Methodist. She consents in writing. p 63

25 November 1805. Benjamin MOORE and Patsey Moody, dau. Jeney Moody. Sur. Absalom Williams. p 153

5 April 1810. Benjamin MOORE and Polly Vaughan. Married by the Rev. Peter Wynne. Ministers' Returns p 389

22 August 1791. Edward MOORE and Caty Seward, dau. John Seward. Sur. Thomas Washington. Wit. Frederick Hobbs and Isham Harrison. Married 30 August by the Rev. Edward Dromgoole. p 65

3 April 1774. James MOORE and Sarah Johnson, dau. Moses Johnson who is surety. Wit. Moses Johnson, Jr. p 15

24 February 1800. James MOORE and Martha Hearn, 21. Sur. William Whitby. Wit. Balaam Ezell. p 119

18 October 1810. James MOORE and Lucy Bass. Sur. Benjamin Bass. p 177

21 June 1799. Jesse MOORE and Elizabeth Peace. Married by the Rev. Peter Wynne. Ministers' Returns p 372

23 February 1807. John F. MOORE and Nancy A. Fletcher. Sur. James N. Fletcher. Married 25 February by the Rev. Edward Dromgoole. p 161

10 April 1799. Littleberry MOORE and Lucy Peace. Married by the Rev. Peter Wynne. Ministers' Returns p 372

17 December 1804. Richard MOORE and Susanna Foster, dau. Elizabeth Foster. Sur. Peter R. Foster. p 148

5 December 1785. Samuel MOORE and Salley Jones. Married by the Rev. John King, Baptist. Ministers' Returns p 351

28 January 1788. Sterling MOORE and Sarah Edwards, 21, dau. Prissy Edwards. Sur. Jesse Braswell. Wit. Isham Edwards and Drury Nanny. Married 3 February by the Rev. John King, Baptist. p 49

8 January 1798. Thomas MOORE, Jr. and Mary Thompson, 21, lived in County 6 months. Sur. Alexander Andrews. Wit. Thomas Morre, Sr., and Martha Moore. Married 10 January by the Rev. Aaron Brown, Methodist. p 103

24 January 1803. Thomas MOORE and Rhoda Manney, 21. Sur. Drury Nanney. Returned 10 March by the Rev. Ira Ellis. p 139

11 May 1795. William MOORE and Frances Miskell. Sur. Jeremiah Miskell. Married 21 May by the Rev. Peter Wynne. p 85

17 July 1797. William MOORE and Frankey Justice, dau. William Justice. Sur. Willie Wesson. Wit. George H. Jones. Married 20 July by the Rev. Edward Dromgoole. p 102

26 November 1798. William MOORE and Priscilla Harris, 21. Sur. John Walton. Sit. Stephen Barnes. Married 6 December by the Rev. Balaam Ezell, Baptist. p 108

13 December 1800. William MOORE and Nancy Hampton. Sur. Jeremiah Hampton. Wit. Peter Potts. p 124

22 December 1788. Francis MORELAND and Hannah Rivers, consent of Thomas Rivers. Sur. Arthur Harrup. p 52

Returned 4 February 1790. John MORGAN and Mary Pool. Married by the Rev. John King, Baptist. Ministers' Returns p 357

3 December 1785. Samuel MORGAN and Sally Jones, dau. Anne Jones, widow.
Sur. Buckner Stith, Jr. p 36

15 January 1807. Stephen MORGAN and Nancy Malone. Married by the Rev.
Peter Wynne. Ministers' Returns p 384

17 November 1783. Thomas MORGAN and Elizabeth Maclin, dau. Henry
Maclin. Sur. James Maclin. p 31

24 January 1803. Benjamin MORRIS and Martha Clayton. This is an error;
the original bond says Benjamin Harris. See Benjamin Harris.
Brunswick p 130

10 March 1810. Benjamin S. MORRIS and Nancy Dugger, 21. Sur. James
Dugger. p 175

24 September 1810. Edward MORRIS and Dolly Edwards, dau. Brambley
Edwards. Sur. Jesse Edwards. Wit. Edward Morris. p 176

26 December 1785. Henry MORRIS and Mason Simmons. Sur. Thomas Smith.
of St. Andrew's Parish. Married by the Rev. Thomas Lundie. p 37

6 November 1805. Isarel MORRIS and Lucy Sturdivant. See Israel Mairs.
Brunswick p 130

22 August 1782. John MORRIS and Elizabeth Edwards, dau. Thomas Edwards,
deceased. Sur. Meredith Poythress, who makes affidavit that
Elizabeth Edwards lives at the home of his father Thomas Poythress
and is 23 years of age. Wit. Griffin Stith. p 29

16 December 1784. Lester MORRIS and Frances Brown, dau. Lewis Brown.
Sur. Lewis Brown, Jr. p 34

9 September 1794. Robert MORRIS and Sally Thompson, 21. Sur. John
Christian. Wit. William Singleton and Robert Thompson. Married
11 September by the Rev. Aaron Brown, Methodist. p 82

22 July 1809. Robert MORRIS and Martha Floyd. Sur. James Ivy. p 172

24 December 1789. Henry MORRISS and Patience Berry. Married by the
Rev. Aaron Brown, Methodist. Ministers' Returns p 355

18 December 1798. Sherrod MORRISS and Amy Floyd, 21. Sur. Morris
Floyd. Wit. James Davis. Married 20 December by the Rev. John
Neblett. p 109

27 September 1807. Cuddy MOSELY and Nelly Mosely, dau. Samuel Moseley.
Sur. Willis Harrison. Married 30 September by the Rev. Edward
Dromgoole, who says Candy Moseley. p 163

2 January 1797. Stephen MOSELEY and Nancy Gunn, dau. William Gunn.
Sur. Peter Read. Married 5 January by the Rev. Balaam Ezell,
Baptist. p 95

24 November 1788. Thomas MOSELEY and Tabitha Bithshears, 21 dau. Thomas Bithshears. Sur. John Moseley. Wit. James Huff. Married by the Rev. John King, Baptist. p 51

24 August 1801. Nichodemus MOSLEY and Tabitha Mosley. Sur. Benjamin Mosley. Returned 24 September by the Rev. Balaam Ezell, Baptist. p 128

27 September 1807. Marcellus MOSS and Olive Huff. Sur. William Huff. Married 6 October by the Rev. Edward Dromgoole. p 163

28 October 1799. Wilkins MOSS and Anna Jackson, dau. Ephraim Jackson. Sur. Randle Jackson. Wit. Thomas Phillips. Married by the Rev. Ira Ellis. p 114

6 May 1798. Sampson MURDOCK and Ann Allgood, 21. Sur. Lewis Saunders. Married by the Rev. William Brown. p 105

28 September 1756. William MURPHY and Lucy Hickman. Sur. George Summers. p 3

12 June 1797. John MURRELL and Rebecca Hardaway, 21. Sur. Benajah Saxon. Married by the Rev. Aaron Brown, Methodist. p 98

- February 1786. Jeffrey MUSTRON and Elizabeth Stegal. Married by the Rev. John King, Baptist. Minsters' Returns p 349

21 April 1791. Christopher MC CONNICO and Mary Stith. Sur. Peter Jones. Wit. Jared McConnico, Jr., and David Jackson. Married by the Rev. Thomas Lundie, Rector of St. Andrew's Parish. p 65

28 December 1799. Cad MC CULLICK and Dolly Rideout, 21. Sur. James Rideout. Wit. William Rideout and Gordan Rideout. Married by the Rev. Aaron Brown, Methodist. p 117

3 March 1788. John MC DANIEL and Betsey Collier, ward of John McDaniel. Sur. Richard Stone. Wit. Sack Pennington. p 49

27 January 1782. James MC INVALE and Jane Stainback, dau. Francis Stainback, deceased. Sur. Edmund Webb. p 28

25 April 1786. James MC INVALE and Mary Woodrough. Sur. Zachariah Sims. Married 5 May by the Rev. John King, Baptist who says Mackenvaille and Woodruff. p 38

26 March 1804. Ebenezer M. MC ROBERTS and Henrietta M. Field. Sur. Thomas Simmons. Wit. John Short. Married 13 April by the Rev. Wright Tucker, Episcopal Rector. p 146

Returned 4 February 1790. Robert NANCE and Fatha Pennington. Married by the Rev. John King, Baptist. Ministers' Returns p 357

5 January 1810. Abel NANNY and Mary Justice, 21. Sur. John Justice. Wit. Isaac Wesson, Jr. Married 11 January by the Rev. Cary James, Methodist. p 174

26 November 1810. Daniel NANNY and Patsy Taylor, 21, dau. Elizabeth
    Taylor. Sur. Drury Barner. Married 28 November by the Rev. Cary
    James, Methodist. p 177

3 December 1800. Jordan Nanny and Oney Gregory, 21. Sur. Pleasant
    Smith. Wit. Isaac Wesson. Married by the Rev. Balaam Ezell,
    Baptist. p 124

26 July 1790. Shade NANNEY and Mary Wright, dau. John Wright. Sur.
    Harwood Clary. Wit. Edmund Webb and John Hoskins. Married
    29 July by the Rev. John King, Baptist. p 60

24 February 1794. Cudbeath (Cuthbert) NEAL and Nancy Powell, ward of
    Thomas Powell who is surety. Wit. Willis Jones, Robert Powell and
    Mason Blanks. Married 27 February by the Rev. Aaron Brown,
    Methodist. p 80

5 August 1769. John NEAL and Susanna Smith, dau. Cuthbert Smith. Sur.
    Charles Smith. Wit. Ann Smith and Edward Fisher. Will, Brunswick
    County 1791. p 7

24 December 1798. John NEAL and Milly Dudley House, dau. Jordan Howse.
    Sur. Isaac Flood House. Wit. Enos Scarbrough, Claiborne Howse and
    Jordan Howse. Married 25 December by the Rev. Balaam Ezell, Baptist.
    p 109

2 December 1805. Capt. Edward NEBLETT and Ann H. Roberts, dau. Samuel
    Roberts. Sur. Sterling Neblett. Married 5 December by the Rev.
    Peter Wynne. p 153

8 May 1792. Abner NEWMAN and Dorothy Steagall. Sur. Thomas Steagall.
    p 70

22 January 1798. Barham NEWSOM and Elizabeth Howard. Sur. Mordecai
    Howard. p 103

12 December 1806. Barham NEWSOM and Catherine Penn, 21. Sur. Thomas
    Marks. Married 13 December by the Rev. Aaron Brown, Methodist. p 159

7 February 1804. Thomas NIBLETT and Polly Williams. Married by the Rev.
    Peter Wynne. Ministers' Returns p 382

7 December 1795. Allan NIPPER and Nancy Griffith, 21. Sur. Thomas
    Griffith. Wit. Thomas Clark. p 88

28 June 1757. John NIVERSON and Anne Tazewell, under 21. John Niverson
    her guardian. Sur. Archibald Wager. Wit. N. Edwards, Jr. p 4

30 January 1810. Alexander NOBLES and Rebecca Clayton, of age. Sur.
    Richard Trotter. p 174

13 January 1798. James NOLLY and Martha Seward. Sur. John Seward.
    Married 23 January by the Rev. James Meacham. p 103

17 August 1793.   John NOLLY and Nancy Dance.   Sur. Nathaniel Lucas.
Wit. Mayes Tarpley and Sally Dance.   p 76

21 March 1804.   Josiah NOLLY and Martha Vaughan.   Married by the Rev.
Aaron Brown, Methodist.   Ministers' Returns   p 386

20 March 1804.   Joseph (or Josiah) NOLLY and Patsey Vaughan.   Sur.
George Vaughan.   p 146

16 April 1810.   Nehemiah NOLLEY and Sally Wynne, 21.   Sur. William B.
Wynne.   Wit. Peter Wynne.   Married 18 April by the Rev. Peter
Wynne.   p 175

24 May 1802. Neverson NOLLEY and Fanny Seward.   Sur. James Nolley.   p 134

4 December 1801.   Richard NOLLEY and Nancy Marks, 21.   Sur. Richardson
Brown.   Wit. Rebecca Brown and Samuel Marks.   Married 17 December by
the Rev. Aaron Brown, Methodist.   p 130

24 January 1804.   Thomas NOLLY and Mary Sadler.   Sur. John Rose.
Married 25 January by the Rev. Aaron Brown, Methodist.   p 145

13 July 1805.   Thomas NOLLY and Rebecca Rogers.   Sur. John Rogers.
Married 17 July by the Rev. Aaron Brown, Methodist.   p 151

28 December 1789.   John NORWARD and Sarah Morris.   Sur. Thomas Morris.
Wit. Charles B. Jones and Joseph Wilkins.   Married by the Rev. John
King, Baptist.   p 57

22 May 1786.   Benjamin OGBORNE and Martha Davis.   Sur. William Ogborne.
Married by the Rev. Thomas Lundie, Rector of St. Andrew's Parish.
p 39

26 March 1787.   Benjamin OGBURN and Sally Cook, 21.   Sur. Robert Morriss.
Wit. William Ogborne.   Married in April 1787 by the Rev. Thomas
Lundie, Rector of St. Andrew's Parish.   p 44

24 March 1809.   Henry W. OGBORNE and Lucy Perry.   Sur. John Taylor. p 171

25 February 1771.   William OGBORNE and Hannah Warren.   Sur. Benjamin
Warren.   p 9

4 February 1799.   Bishop OLDHAM and Elizabeth Hampton, over 21.   Sur.
Charles Oldham.   Wit. Jeremiah Hampton.   Married 7 February by the
Rev. Peter Wynne.   p 111

16 November 1796.   Charles OLDHAM and Patsey Wynne, dau. Peter Wynne, Sr.
Sur. Peter Wynne, Jr. Wit. Richard Oldham.   Married 17 November by
the Rev. Peter Wynne.   p 92

29 December 1786.   Isaac OLDHAM and Winifred Tarpley.   Sur. Charles
Tarpley.   p 43

- December 1786.   Richard OLDHAM and Winefred Tarpley.   Married by the
Rev. Thomas Lundie, Rector of St. Andrew's Parish.   Ministers'
Returns   p 350

23 December 1799. Richard OLDHAM and Eliza Mairs or Mares. Sur. John Stith. Married 24 December by the Rev. Henry Merritt. p 117

13 January 1802. Richard OLDHAM and Tabitha Rives, 21. Sur. Miles Collier. Married 14 January by the Rev. Aaron Brown, Methodist. p 132

10 December 1802. John ORGAIN and Polley Birchett. Sur. Clement Mitchell. Married 11 December by the Rev. Aaron Brown, Methodist. p 137

18 May 1802. Littleberry ORGAIN and Polley G. Johnson. Sur. Benjamin Johnson. Married 19 May by the Rev. John Neblett. p 134

23 June 1803. William ORGAIN and Salley Meredith. Sur. Thomas Orgain. p 141

25 November 1799. Richard OSMORE and Susanna Wade, 21. Sur. Thomas Wade. Wit. David Elder and Edward Taylor. p 115

- September 1785. Jeremiah OVERBY and Mary Flood (?) of Bath Parish. Married by the Rev. Thomas Lundie, Rector of St. Andrew's Parish. Ministers' Returns p 345

26 August 1805. Thomas OVERBY and Martha Sykes. Sur. Jesse Peebles. Married 7 September by the Rev. Peter Wynne. p 151

5 December 1791. Abner OWEN and Frances Davenport, dau. Mary Davenport. Sur. John Owen. Wit. Thomas Owen. Married 8 December by the Rev. Aaron Brown, Methodist. p 66

22 July 1805. Bolling OWEN and Betsey Wesson, 21. Sur. John Wesson, Wit. John Lightfoot. p 151

26 June 1786. James OWEN and Anne Wilkes, dau. John Wilkes, deceased. Sur. Burwell Wilkes. p 39

22 October 1788. John OWEN and Mary Stainback, dau. Littleberry Stainback, deceased, and Lucy Stainback. Sur. John Stainback. Married by the Rev. Thomas Lundie, Rector of St. Andrew's Parish who says Nancy. p 51

20 December 1801. John OWEN and Nancy Williams. Sur. William Williams. p 131

20 October 1789. Richard B. OWEN and Susanna Edwards, dau. Capt. William Edwards, deceased. John Hardaway, guardian. Consent of Susanna Simmons. Sur. Gronow Owen. Wit. Susanna Tilman and Mary Tillman. Married by the Rev. Thomas Lundie, Rector of St. Andrew's p 56

22 December 1778. Robert OWEN and Sarah Richardson, dau. William Richardson. Sur. Lewis Brown. Wit. Charles Harrison and John Smith. p 21

23 November 1795. Robert OWEN and Mary Mathis (or Mathews); Nelly
Mathews makes affidavit as to her age. Sur. Arthur Frost. Wit.
Alexander Andrews and Anderson Andrews. Married 24 November by
the Rev. Aaron Brown, Methodist. p 87

15 October 1803. Robert OWEN and Polley Lanier, 21. Sur. Thomas
Lanier. Wit. Drury Lanier. p 142

28 February 1803. Sterling OWEN and Lurana Brewer, of age. Sur.
Phillip Owen. Returned 16 March by the Rev. Ira Ellis. p 140

25 December 1804. Thomas OWENS and Polly Lane, dau. Micajah Lane.
Sur. Thomas Lane. Married 26 December by the Rev. Edward Dromgoole.
p 149

22 December 1806. William OWENS and Lucy Wright. Sur. Samuel Wright.
Married 23 December by the Rev. Hubbard Saunders. p 159

26 November 1769. John PACE and Ann Russell. Sur. John Russell. p 7

20 December 1804. Edward PALMER and Sally Jones. Married by the Rev.
Peter Wynne. Ministers' Returns p 382

24 November 1806. William PALMER and Catherine Maclin, dau. Joseph
Maclin. Sur. Thomas Morgan. Wit. Polley M. Morgan. Married 27
November by the Rev. Aaron Brown, Methodist. p 159

28 April 1770. Ephraim PARHAM and Ann Collier, dau. Thomas Collier who
is surety. Wit. Edward Fisher. p 8

23 November 1778. Ephraim PARHAM and Parthenia Gee, dau. William Gee.
Sur. John Maclin. p 20

19 April 1794. Ephraim PARHAM and Frances Harrison, ward of Richard B.
Owen. Sur. Benjamin Smith. Wit. Martha Jackson and Susanna Owen.
Married 23 April by the Rev. Aaron Brown, Methodist. p 80

23 October 1778. James PARHAM and -   -   . Sur. Nicholas
Edmunds. p 23

25 November 1755. Matthew PARHAM, Jr. and Rebecca Maclin. Sur. John
Maclin. p 2

22 July 1777. Thomas PARHAM and Elizabeth Gilliam; William Mason,
guardian of both, is surety. p 17

20 June 1771. William PARHAM and Hannah Hill, widow. Sur. Francis
Young. Wit. Elizabeth Young, John Sims, Nathaniel Mabry and James
Denton. p 9

31 January 1805. James PARISH and Elizabeth Kirkland. Married by the
Rev. Hubbard Saunders. Ministers' Returns p 383

7 January 1797. Jones PARISH and Vicey Rawlings, 21, dau. Sally
Rawlings. Sur. Henry Rawlings. Wit. John Rawlings. Married by
the Rev. Aaron Brown, Methodist. p 95

11 October 1795. Matthew PARISH and Margaret Lawler, 22, Robert
Kennedy makes affidavit as to her age. Sur. Robert Duncan. Wit.
Jane Kennedy and Patty Kennedy. p 86

28 January 1798. William PARISH and Jean Canady. Sur. Robert Kennedy.
Wit. Robert Canady. p 104

31 December 1810. William PARISH and Susanna Dean (Jane Dane)? (sic).
Sur. Edward Morriss. p 178

1 February 1806. Henry PARRISH and Polly Whitt, 21. Sur. Shadrack
Brewer. Married by the Rev. Hubbard Saunders. p 155

27 February 1807. Thomas PARSONS and Jamima Holloway. Married by the
Rev. Peter Wynne. Ministers' Returns p 384

12 February 1808. Wiley PARSONS and Lucy Wells. Married by the Rev.
Peter Wynne. Ministers' Returns p 384

25 August 1806. King PATTERSON and Polly Rawlings. Sur. Randle Rawlings. Married by the Rev. Hubbard Suanders. p 157

22 February 1790. John PAUP and Sarah H. Walker. Sur. Thomas Stith, Sr.
Wit. John Jones. p 58

27 October 1789. Richard PEARCEY and Elizabeth Grubbs. Married by the
Rev. Aaron Brown, Methodist. See Richard Pierce, also, Richard
Pucey. p 56

30 August 1795. Sherwood PEARCY and Martha Crook. Married by the Rev.
Peter Wynne. Ministers' Returns p 364

23 July 1781. James PEARSON and Susanna Day, dau. Oliver Day. Sur.
Briggs Goodrich. p 26

22 February 1792. James PEARSON and Mary Walton, widow. Sur. George
Walton. Wit. John Walton, Gregory Johnson and George Walton, Jr.
James Pearson of Greenville County. Married 23 February by the
Rev. Edward Dromgoole. p 69

27 October 1794. John PEARSON and Martha Britt, 21. Sur. Henry Britt.
Wit. Isaac Britt. Married 30 October by the Rev. Edward Dromgoole.
p 82

27 September 1801. John PEARSON and Rebecca Wright, 21. Sur. John
Wright. Married 5 November by the Rev. Ira Ellis. p 135

18 December 1805. Johnson PEARSON and Sally Brewer. Sur. Kinchen
Brewer. p 153

- November 1786. Littleberry PEARSON and Mary Thomas. Married by
the Rev. Thomas Lundie, Rector of St. Andrew Parish. Ministers'
Returns. p 349

5 March 1800. Littleton PEARSON and Sally Brewer, of age. Sur. Berryman Ezell. Wit. Mors. Pearson, Benjamin King, Henry King and
John Brewer. p 120

22 December 1788. Morris PEARSON and Nancy Brewer. Sur. John Brewer.
p 52

28 February 1799. William PEARSON and Ann Floyd. Sur. Littleberry
(or Littleton) Pearson. Wit. Benjamin King. Married 1 March by
the Rev. Edward Dromgoole. p 111

8 January 1800. Allan G. PEEBLES and Polly Smith, dau. Stephen Smith.
Sur. Harrison Smith. Wit. Sterling Smith. p 119

7 December 1807. Alen G. PEEBLES and Elizabeth Stainback. Sur. William
Stainback. Married 9 December by the Rev. Aaron Brown, Methodist.
p 165

22 December 1779. Drury PEEBLES and Lucy Wilburn. Sur. John Peebles,
Jr. p 23

22 September 1806. Jesse PEEBLES and Elizabeth Lanier, 21. Sur. Thomas
Lanier. Married 4 October by the Rev. Peter Wynne. p 157

23 April 1810. Jesse PEEBLES and Martha Williams, 21. Sur. Bradford
Burge. Wit. William Penticost and David Jackson. p 175

28 November 1758. Joseph PEEBLES and Mary Roberson, or Robinson, under
21. Sur. Archibald Wager. p 5

25 January 1779. Lewis PEEBLES and Jean Hicks. Lewis son of David
Peebles who consents. Sur. Robert Hicks. Wit. Hubbard Peebles
and John Peebles. p 21

July 1787 - July 1788. Sterling PEEPLES and Patsy Wilkins. Married by
the Rev. Thomas Lundie, Rector of St. Andrew's Parish. Ministers'
Returns p 352

21 September 1804. William PEEBLES and Elizabeth Potts, 21. Sur.
William Major. Married 4 October by the Rev. Peter Wynne. p 147

- August 1785. Daniel PEGRAM and Nancy Hardaway, both of Bath Parish.
Married by the Rev. Thomas Lundie, Rector of St. Andrew's Parish.
Ministers' Returns p 345

24 June 1799. Edward PEGRAM, Jr. and Rebecca Harper, ward of Richard
Coleman. Sur. Thomas Manson. Married 11 July by the Rev. Peter
Wynne. p 112

11 April 1791. Nathan PENICK and Elizabeth Fowlks, dau. Thomas Fowlks.
Sur. Joseph Browder. Wit. John Fowlks, Sr., and William Hamblin.
Married by the Rev. Aaron Brown, Methodist. p 65

18 December 1786. Jesse PENN and Charlotte Ingram. Sur. Bartho. Ingram.
Married by the Rev. Thomas Lundie, Rector of St. Andrew's Parish.
p 42

30 November 1786. John PENN and Mary Briggs, 21. Sur. Reuben Wright.
Wit. Bartholomew Ingram. Married by the Rev. Thomas Lundie, Rector
of St. Andrew's Parish. p 42

26 October 1804. Pascal PENN and Sally Orgain. Sur. Green Hill.
Married 29 October by the Rev. Aaron Brown, Methodist. p 148

3 December 1804. Thomas PENN and Tabitha Lucas, dau. Frederick Lucas.
Sur. Herbert Hill. Married 6 December by the Rev. Aaron Brown,
Methodist. p 148

10 May 1802. John Thomas PENNINGTON and Betsy Pennington. Sur. William
T. Pennington. Married 18 May by the Rev. Aaron Brown, Methodist.
p 133

27 - 1786. Robert PENNINGTON and Frances Tinch or Linch. Married
by the Rev. John King, Baptist. Ministers' Returns p 349

30 June 1795. William Thomas PENNINGTON and Mary Clarke. Sur. Benajah
Saxon. Married by the Rev. Aaron Brown, Methodist. p 86

27 July 1799. William PENNINGTON and Nancy Murrell. Sur. John Murrell.
Married 2 August by the Rev. Aaron Brown, Methodist. Wit. William
Murrell. p 113

24 February 1787. James PENTICOST and Sally Saunders. Sur. Ebbin
Saunders. Brunswick says Lucy Saunders which is an error; original
bond says Sally Saunders. p 43

15 October 1810. William PENTICOST and Dorothy Coleman, dau. Richard
Coleman. Sur. David Jackson. Wit. Henry W. Coleman. p 176

14 September 1786. Richard PEPPER and Subina Connoly, 21, dau. Sarah
Connoly. Sur. Lewis Connoly. Wit. Mils Houze and William Houze.
Married by the Rev. Thomas Lundie, Rector of St. Andrew's Parish.
p 40

28 November 1796. William B. PEPPER and Polly Williams. Sur. George
Williams. Married by the Rev. Peter Wynne. p 93

11 September 1799. Joseph PERCIVALL and Peggy Love, of age. Sur.
Thomas Washington. Wit. Lucy Robinson. Married by the Rev. James
Meacham. p 114

23 March 1807. Gideon PERKINS and Elizabeth Jesse. Sur. Young D.
Perkins. Wit. John Robertson. p 161

22 December 1800. Young D. PERKINS and Lavinia Lucy, dau. Rachel Lucy.
Sur. Gardner Scoggins. Wit. Moody Vaughan. Married 25 December by
the Rev. Peter Wynne. p 124

6 September 1790. Archibald PERKINSON and Amy Harwell, 21. Sur. Isham
Perkinson. Wit. Richard B. Owen. Married by the Rev. Thomas Lundie,
Rector of St. Andrew's Parish. p 60

9 July 1798. Seth PERKINSON and Keziah Curtis, 21. Sur. Robert Hardaway. Wit. Nathaniel Collier. Married 11 July by the Rev. Balaam
Ezell, Baptist. p 106

28 January 1778. Julius PERRY and Lucy Charles, dau. Lewis Charles.
Sur. Lewis Charles, Jr. Wit. Robert Spencer and William Charles.
p 18

20 December 1805. Jesse PETERSON and Hannah Vaughan. Sur. James
Vaughan. Married 21 December by the Rev. Aaron Brown, Methodist.
p 153

11 June 1795. Laban PETILLO and Betsy Reese. Sur. Isham Reese. p 86

27 April 1803. Laban PETILLO and Caty Stone, 21, dau. Margaret Stone.
Sur. Lewis Lambert. Wit. John Stone and Peter Stone. p 140

20 October 1809. Laban PETILLO and Mary Smith. Sur. Bottom Steagall.
Returned 16 November by the Rev. Peter Wynne. p 172

2 February 1798. Littlejohn PETILLO and Judith Barner. Sur. John
Barner. Married 15 February by the Rev. James Meacham. p 104

24 March 1800. John PETILLO and Patsey Steed, dau. Mark and Caty
Steed. Sur. Jeduthan Steed. Married 3 April by the Rev. James
Meacham. p 120

- September 1785. John PETTYPOOL and Rebecca Wilkinson of Albermarle
Parish. Married by the Rev. Thomas Lundie, Rector of St. Andrew's
Parish. Ministers' Returns p 345

- December 1785. Seth PETTYPOOL and Lucretia Winfield of Albermarle
Parish. Married by the Rev. Thomas Lundie, Rector of St. Andrew's
Ministers' Returns p 346

20 November 1786. Frederick PHENIX and Patty Overby. Sur. Joel Biggs.
See Drury Phoenix. p 42

12 August 1806. Frederick PHOENIX, Jr. and Elizabeth Phoenix, dau.
Frederick Phoenix. Sur. John Phoenix. Brunswick says 1808.
Married 14 August 1806 by the Rev. Peter Wynne. p 157

Between July 1787 and July 1788. Drury PHEONIX and Paty Overby.
Married by the Rev. Thomas Lundie, Rector of St. Andrew's Parish.
See Frederick Phenix. Ministers' Returns p 351

5 November 1787. Thomas PHILIPS and Anne Clark, dau. John Clark.
Sur. Robert Brister. Wit. Henry Mangum. p 47

3 December 1792. Sterling PHILLIPS and Mary Williams, of age. Sur.
Henry Wesson. Wit. John Wesson and John Stacy. p 72

6 February 1796. William PHILLIPS and Nancy James, 21. Sur. Cary
James. Wit. George H. Jones, Abner Woolsey and Hicks Jones.
Married by the Rev. Edward Dromgoole 9 February. p 90

16 February 1791. Benjamin PHIPPS and Lucy Turbefield, 21. Sur. David
Kirkland. Wit. William Turbyfield and Richardson Phipps. Married
19 February by the Rev. Aaron Brown, Methodist, who says Turbyfill.
p 64

27 October 1789. Richard PIERCE and Elizabeth Grubbs, 21, dau. Susanna
Grubbs. Sur. Richard Biggs. Wit. Clement Read and Lucy Briggs.
See Richard Pearcey also Richard Pucey. p 56

18 September 1792. Joseph PORTER and Penelope Gee, dau. William Gee
who is surety. Wit. William Collier. p 71

29 January 1790. Samuel PORTER and Hannah Gee. Sur. William Gee.
Married by the Rev. John King, Baptist. p 58

3 December 1786. George POTTS and Anne Daniel, dau. Ann Daniel, Sr.
Sur. Jesse Potts. Married by the Rev. Thomas Lundie, Rector of
St. Andrew's Parish. p 42

5 March 1789. Nathan POTTS and Betsy Dixon. Sur. Samuel Steagall.
Married by the Rev. Thomas Lundie, Rector of St. Andrew's Parish. p 53

30 May 1797. Solomon POTTS and Elizabeth Daniel, 21. Sur. Nathan Potts.
Wit. Peter Potts. Married 4 June by the Rev. John Rogers. p 98

12 March 1798. Edward POWELL and Eliza Tilman, 21. Sur. John Harrison.
Wit. Stephen Smith. Married 15 March by the Rev. Edward Dromgoole.
p 104

22 December 1788. James POWELL and Nancy Gholson, dau. Thomas Gholson.
Sur. William Stainback. Wit. James Johnson. p 52

22 April 1801. James POWELL and Sally Lashley, dau. Elizabeth Lashley.
Sur. Herbert Hill. Married 23 April by the Rev. Edward Dromgoole.
p 127

24 December 1754. John POWELL and Sarah Parish, widow. Sur. Lucas
Powell. Wit. Miles Cary. p 2

9 April 1799. John POWELL and Sally Powell, 21. Sur. Thomas Powell.
Wit. Edward Powell. Married 10 April by the Rev. Aaron Brown,
Methodist. p 112

25 September 1751. Seymour POWELL and Frances Peterson, widow. Sur.
Lewis Parham. p 1

27 January 1800. Seymore POWELL and Polly Powell, 21. Sur. John Stainback. Wit. W. H. Powell. Married by the Rev. Aaron Brown,
Methodist. p 119

27 November 1798. Thomas POWELL and Patsey Lashley. Married by the Rev.
Aaron Brown, Methodist. Ministers' Returns p 368

14 February 1797. Henry F. POWER and Polly Harrison, 21. Sur. James
Harrison. Wit. Willie Harrison. Married by the Rev. James
Meacham who says Mary. p 97

24 August 1789. John PRICE and Suckey Proctor. Sur. Daniel Dugger. Married by the Rev. Aaron Brown, Methodist. p 55

22 November 1784. Joseph PRICE and Luvany Dugger. Sur. John Dugger, Jr. p 34

28 July 1789. Richard PRICE and Obedience Edwards, 21. Sur. Daniel Dugger. Wit. John Price. Married by the Rev. Aaron Brown, Methodist. p 55

23 December 1805. Thomas D. PRICE and Polly Edmunds. Sur. Nicholas Edmunds. p 154

22 April 1799. Thomas PRIDE and Lucy Scott. Married by the Rev. Peter Wynne. Ministers' Returnes p 372

18 October 1779. Joel PRINCE and Mary (or Mourning) Avent, dau. William Avent. Sur. Thomas Jordan. Wit. Churchill Anderson and Thomas Camp. p 22

24 September 1787. John PRINCE and Elizabeth Freeman, dau. Jesse Freeman who is surety. Wit. John Powell p 46

26 November 1798. Caleb PRITCHETT and Sally Howerton, 21. Sur. Drury Howerton. Wit. John Davis. Returned 4 January 1799 by the Rev. Peter Wynne. p 108

3 December 1799. Edward PRITCHETT and Rebecca Westmoreland, consent of Martha Westmoreland. Sur. Robert Westmoreland. Wit. Thomas Jolly. Married 5 December by the Rev. Aaron Brown, Methodist. p 116

9 February 1805. Edwin PRITCHETT and Polly Elmore. Sur. William Brown. Married 20 February by the Rev. Aaron Brown, Methodist. p 150

22 February 1802. Jesse PRITCHETT and Ruth Westmoreland. This is an error. Original bond says Jesse Puckett. See Jesse Puckett. Brunswick p 150

29 July 1799. Joseph T. PRITCHETT and Winifred Williams, 21. Sur. Thomas Barker. Wit. Burwell Barker and John Barker. Married 31 July by the Rev. James Meacham who says Joseph L. Brunswick says Joseph J. p 113

23 April 1807. Moses PRITCHETT and Martha Celey. Sur. Wilson B. Celey. p 165

25 December 1805. William PRITCHETT and Susan Davis, 21. Sur. Edmund Pritchett. Married 27 December by the Rev. Aaron Brown, Methodist. p 154

20 March 1788. Joshua PROCTOR and Charity Edwards, widow. Sur. David Dugger. p 50

2 August 1808. Luke Pryor and Nancy Lane. Sur. Edmund Shell. p 167

5 July 1802. Phillip PRYOR and Susan C. Wilkes. Sur. Burwell Wilkes.
p 134

27 October 1789. Richard PUCEY and Elizabeth Grubbs. See Richard
Pearcey and Richard Pierce. Brunswick p 152

22 February 1802. Jesse PUCKETT and Ruth Westmoreland. Sur. Griffin
Stith. Married 27 February by the Rev. Peter Wynne. p 133

- December 1786. David PUTNEY and Mary Wyche. Married by the Rev.
Thomas Lundie, Rector of St. Andrew's Parish. This bond is in
Sussex County. Ministers' Returns p 350

9 February 1807. Benjamin QUARLES and Nancy Cattles, 21. Sur. John
Quarles. Wit. Nancy Moore and Polly Roper. Married 10 February
by the Rev. Peter Wynne. p 161

27 July 1785. Croxton QUARLES and Elizabeth Piercy. Sur. Peter
Wynne. Of St. Andrew's Parish, married by the Rev. Thomas Lundie.
p 35

27 October 1802. James QUARLES and Mary Ann Brown, consent of William
Brown. Sur. William Rash. Married 30 October by the Rev. Peter
Wynne. p 136

14 August 1804. John QUARLES and Martha Burge. Sur. Wood Burge.
Married 18 August by the Rev. Peter Wynne. p 147

23 March 1778. Moses QUARLES and Constance Fisher. Sur. James Fisher.
p 19

11 October 1796. William QUARLES and Sally Dance, 21. Sur. William
Elmore. Wit. John Allen. p 92

13 January 1802. Francis RACHEL and Silvia Barnes, dau. William Barnes.
Sur. James Barnes. Wit. William Makaney, Jr. Married 16 January
by the Rev. Aaron Brown, Methodist. p 132

23 February 1784. William RAGSDALE and Anne Scarbrough, dau. Edward
Scarbrough, deceased. Sur. Lewis Scarbrough. p 32

28 January 1788. Christopher RAINES and Anny Baird, dau. John Baird.
Sur. William Mitchell. Married by the Rev. John King, Bpatist who
says Anne Beard. p 49

24 April 1780. Hartwell RAINES and Rebecca Lucas. Sur. John Lucas. p 24

18 May 1796. Nathaniel RAINES and Susan Parham, ward of James Banks.
Sur. John Wyche. Wit. Philip Claiborne. p 90

6 February 1809. Benjamin L. RAINEY and Elizabeth Short, 21. Sur.
Alexander Nobles. Married 9 February by the Rev. Peter Wynne. 1 170

26 May 1800. Francis RAINEY and Nancy Wilson, dau. John Wilson. Sur.
James Rainey. Wit. John Green, Jonathan Fisher and Richard Coleman.
Married by the Rev. Peter Wynne. p 120

25 November 1799. James RAINEY and Susanna Kirkland, 21. Sur. William
Kirkland. Married 30 November by the Rev. Aaron Brown, Methodist.
p 115

16 April 1799. Jesse RAINEY and Frances Duggar, dau. Daniel Duggar.
Sur. Jordan Richardson. Wit. James Stainback. Married 18 April
by the Rev. Aaron Brown, Methodist. p 112

2 March 1809. John RAINEY and Permely Edwards, dau. John Edwards.
Sur. Smith Rainey. Wit. Harbard Hill. p 171

31 March 1797. Nathaniel RAINEY and Catharine House, of age. Henry
Morris, Sr., makes affidavt as to her age. Sur. Herbert Rainey.
Married by the Rev. Hubbard Saunders. p 98

26 October 1795. Zebulan RAINEY and Nancy Loyd, 21. dau. John Loyd.
Sur. Henry Loyd. Wit. Stephen Lloyd and William Rainey, Sr.
Married by the Rev. Aaron Brown, Methodist. p 87

14 July 1798. James RAMSEY and Polly Porter, dau. John Porter. Sur.
Joshua Porter. Wit. Thomas Manson. p 106

28 September 1778. John RANDLE and Tabitha Lyons. Sur. Peter
Randle. p 20

July 1787 - July 1788. Harrison RANDOLPH and Mary Jones. Married by
the Rev. Thomas Lundie, Rector of St. Andrew's Parish. Ministers'
Returns p 351

30 July 1794. Isham RANEY and Sally Firth, 21, dau. Sarah Firth. Sur.
William Firth. Wit. Thomas Firth, Randolph Rawlings and Elizabeth
Rawlings. Married 31 July by the Rev. Aaron Brown, Methodist, who
says Sarah. p 81

16 January 1792. William RANEY and Rebecca White. Sur. Blumer White.
p 69

22 September 1797. William RASH and Elizabeth Brown, consent of William
Brown. Sur. John Brown. Wit. Luke Matthews and Robert Haskins. p 99

July 1789 - July 1790. - RAWLINGS and Clarissa Abernathy. Married
by the Rev. Thomas Lundie, Rector of St. Andrew's Parish.
Ministers' Returns p 356

5 December 1810. Alexander RAWLINGS and Sally Taylor, 21. Sur. John
Seward. Married 6 December by the Rev. Cary James, Methodist. p 178

17 January 1799. Benjamin RAWLINGS and Miner Wilkes, 21. Sur. Herbert
Hill. Wit. Thomas Wilkes and John Fowlkes. Married 24 January by
the Rev. Aaron Brown, Methodist. p 110

21 March 1786. Charles RAWLINGS and Sarah Allen, dau. John Allen. Sur.
Frances Mallory. Married 23 March by the Rev. John King, Baptist,
who says Rollings. p 38

13 February 1807. Daniel RAWLINGS and Clarisa Ann Barnes. Sur. James Barnes. Married 14 February by the Rev. Aaron Brown, Methodist, who says <u>Nancy</u> Barnes. p 161

24 January 1785. Henry RAWLINGS and Sarah Dugger. Sur. Thomas Stith. Married by the Rev. Thomas Lundie, Rector of St. Andrew's Parish, Brunswick County. p 35

25 April 1804. James RAWLINGS and Eliza Jackson. Sur. Green Jackson. p 146

10 October 1803. Littleberry RAWLINGS and Fanny Duggar, 21. Sur. Jordan Richardson. Wit. James Duggar. Married by the Rev. Aaron Brown, Methodist. p 142

26 January 1789. Randle RAWLINGS and Elizabeth Firth, dau. Thomas Firth. Sur. John Williams. p 53

1 December 1804. Claxton RAY and Sally Ray. See Claxton Wray. Brunswick p 156

31 October 1805. Francis RAY and Vyny Linch. Sur. William Linch. See Francis Wray. p 152

26 March 1787. Frederick RAY and Nancy Harwell, dau. Mary Harwell. Sur. Reuben Ray. Wit. Thomas Stith and John Hardaway, Sr. Married by the Rev. John King, Baptist. p 44

18 December 1801. Claxton READ and Oney Huskey, 21. Sur. Cannon Jones. Brunswick says <u>Amey</u>. Married 24 December by the Rev. Edward Dromgoole who says Oney. p 131

27 March 1789. Clement READ and Clarissa Edmunds, dau. Thomas Edmunds. Sur. Edmunds Stith. Wit. Margaret Read and Betty Read. Joel Watkins and Thomas Read guardians of Clement Read. Married by the Rev. Thomas Lundie, Rector of St. Andrew's Parish. p 53

17 November 1796. Clement READ and Amy Malone. Married by the Rev. Peter Wynne. Ministers' Returns p 366

2 January 1810. Jesse READ and Susan Lundie, widow. Wm. & M.Q. 1st Ser. Vol. VII p 38: July 1898

23 December 1799. Robert READ and Polly Brown, 21. Sur. Peter Read. Wit. Radford Gunn. Married by the Rev. Balaam Ezell, Baptist. p 116

20 February 1787. Thomas READ and Nancy QUARLES, dau. James Quarles. Sur. John READE. Married by the Rev. Thomas Lundie, Rector of St. Andrew's Parish. p 43

24 November 1783. William READE and Susanna Grubs, dau. Hensly Grubs, deceased. Sur. Moses Quarles. Married by the Rev. Thomas Lundie, Rector of St. Andrew's Parish. p 31

25 October 1784. Isaac REAVES and Hannah Wallace, dau. John Wallace.
See Isaac Reavis. Brunswick p 156

19 July 1808. Lewis REAVES and Sally Wyche. Sur. Peter B. Wyche. p 167

25 October 1784. Isaac REAVIS and Hannah Wallace, sister of Edward
Wallace who makes affidavit that Hannah is about 24. Isaac Reavis
son of William Reavis. Sur. Edward Wallace. See Isaac Reaves. p 33

2 January 1810. Jesse REED and Susan Lundie. Sur. Herbert Hill.
Married by the Rev. Cary James, Methodist. p 174

26 January 1797. Freeman H. REESE and Fanny Brown. Married by the
Rev. Peter Wynne. Ministers' Returns p 366

11 June 1795. Isham REESE and Ann Cordle, dau. John and Sarah Cordle.
Sur. Laban Potillo. Wit. Charles Berry Jones. Married 17 June by
the Rev. Peter Wynne. p 86

29 May 1800. Joseph REESE and Martha McCan, 21, dau. James and Mary
McCan. Nathan Potts. Married 1 June by the Rev. John Neblett. p 121

29 October 1810. Robert REESE and Lucy M. Weaver. Sur. John Rogers.
Wit. Peter Davis, Jr. and Reuben Cooper. p 177

21 October 1780. Benjamin REIVES, Jr. and Dolly Haley, dau. James
Haley, consent only. p 25

- May 1791. Benjamin RIEVES (or Rives) and Bethea Rosser, widow. Sur.
John Rosser. Wit. W. Edwards and George Little. 20 W (1) 195 says
Bathin. Also, Wm. & M.Q. (1) Vol 28 (1920) p 168. p 23

10 December 1796. Andrew RHEA and Susanna Stith, dau. Thomas Stith, Sr.
Sur. Richard Stith. Wit. David Stith and Peterson Hardaway. p 93

28 June 1799. Randolph RHODES and Phebe Maddox, 21. Sur. Daniel
Pritchett. Wit. Joseph Maclin. p 113

7 November 1796. James RICE and Lucy West. See James Ricce.
Brunswick p 156

18 December 1795. Arthur RICHARDSON and Elizabeth Wright, 21. Sur.
John Wright. Wit. Jarratt Wright. Married 24 December by the Rev.
Edward Dromgoole. p 89

14 December 1798. Jordan RICHARDSON and Susanna Duggar, 21. Sur.
William Fortiscue. Wit. Henry Abernathy. Married 27 December by
the Rev. Aaron Brown, Methodist. p 108

23 April 1810. Thomas RICHARDSON, Jr. and Elizabeth Eaves. Sur.
Nathaniel Green. Married 10 May by the Rev. Cary James, Methodist.
p 175

1 May 1786. William RICHARDSON and Ann Green, widow. Sur. Lewis Brown.
Married by the Rev. Thomas Lundie, Rector of St. Andrew Parish. p 39

6 February 1793. William RICHARDSON and Elizabeth Yeargin, widow of Andrew Yeargin, dau. James Read, Sr. Sur. Pater Read. Married by the Rev. Edward Dromgoole. p 74

24 November 1793. Jiles RIDEOUT and Elizabeth Fort, ward of Isham Smith. Sur. Edward Fort. Married 26 November by the Rev. Aaron Brown, Methodist, who says Giles Rideout. p 77

15 March 1800. John RIDEOUT and Mary Lanier, 21. Sur. Charles Harrison. Wit. Edward Branch. p 120

2 January 1787. Joseph King RIDEOUT and Vickey Barnes, ward of William Rideout. Sur. John Rideout. Wit. William Vaughan and John Gordon Rideout. p 43

19 October 1796. William RIDEOUT and Sarah Harwell, 21. Sur. James Harwell. Wit. William Lanier and Benjamin Lanier. p 92

25 September 1758. James Day RIDLEY and Mary Edwards. Sur. Archibald Wager. Wit. Thomas Simmons. James Day Ridley of Southampton County. p 5

7 November 1796. James RIECE and Lucy West. Sur. Lewis Holloway. See James Rice. p 92

29 September 1783. Thomas RIEVES and Susanna Gee, dau. William Gee. Sur. John Gee. Wit. Francis Thompson and Benjamin Caleb. p 31

27 June 1790. Wyatt RIVEER and Leean Jones. Married by the Rev. John King, Baptist. Ministers' Return p 358

29 May 1791. Timothy RIVERS and Priscilla Turner. See Timothy Rives. Brunswick p 158

- October 1785. Robert RIVERS and Jane Harrison. Married by the Rev. Thomas Lundie, Rector of St. Andrew's Parish. Ministers' Returns p 345

2 December 1801. William RIVERS and Elizabeth Brown. Sur. Aaron Brown. Married by the Rev. John Neblett. p 130

- December 1786. Nathaniel RIVES and Elizabeth Rivers. Married by the Rev. Thomas Lundie, Rector of St. Andrew's Parish. Ministers' Returns p 350

29 December 1772. Timothy RIVES and Priscilla Turner. Sur. Robert Rives. Wit. Peter Pelham, Jr. See Timothy Rivers. p 12

28 January 1799. Abram ROBERD and Betsey Thompson. Sur. Thomas Wade. Returned 19 April by the Rev. Ira Ellis. p 111

13 February 1799. Stephen ROBERTS and Oney Nanny, dau. Amos Nanny who is surety. Brunswick says Amey. Married by the Rev. Balaam Ezell, Baptist. p 111

27 November 1801. Edward ROBERTSON and Rebecca Robertson, consent of
Sterling Peebles (for both?). Sur. James Robertson. Wit. Robert
Peebles and Cadwallader Jones. Married 1 December by the Rev.
Ira Ellis. p 130

25 August 1756. Edward ROBINSON and Anne Cauze, widow. Sur. James
Parhan. Wm. & M. Q. 1st Ser. Vol XX p 195: 1911

30 September 1772. Henry ROBINSON and Mary Clack. Sur. John Clack.
Va. Mag. VOl. XXVIII p 166: April 1920. Wm. & M. Q. 1st Ser. Vol.
VII p 38: July 1898

27 February 1761. James ROBINSON and Winifred Fox. Sur. William Fox.
Wit. Peter Pelham, Jr. Wm & M. Q. 1st Sev. Vol. XX p 195: 1911

22 December 1808. John ROBINSON and Eliza P. Clack. Sur. Edward
Thrower. Married 28 December by the Rev. Edward Dromgoole. p 169

25 November 1790. Littleberry ROBINSON, Jr., and Sally Robinson, dau.
John Robinson. Sur. Lockett Mitchell. Wit. Thomas Mitchell. p 61

23 October 1769. Nathaniel ROBINSON and Eliza Merritt. Sur. Thomas
Mason. Wm. & M. Q. 1st Ser. Vol. XX p 195; 1911

25 November 1805. George ROGERS and Elizabeth Nolly, consent of
Nehemiah Nolly. Sur. Thomas Nolly. Wit. Nehemiah Nolly, Jr., and
Nancy Nolly. Returned 24 December by the Rev. Aaron Brown,
Methodist. p 153

22 October 1787. John ROGERS and Mary Richardson, dau. Thomas
Richardson. Sur. James Penticost. Married by the Rev. Thomas
Lundie, Rector of St. Andrew's Parish. p 46

13 February 1806. John ROGERS and Sally Zachary. Sur. William Crittenden. Wit. James Gunn, Jr. and Elizabeth J. Gunn. p 155

22 December 1785. Jeremiah ROPER and Patsey Wilson, dau. John Wilson.
Sur. Moses Quarles, Jr. Wit. Andrew Meade. Of St. Andrew's
Parish. Married by the Rev. Thomas Lundie. p 37

28 January 1775. John ROSE and Elizabeth Davis. Sur. Benjamin Davis.
Wit. Randol Davis and Hannah Marriott. p 16

7 December 1801. John ROSE and Elizabeth Talley. Sur. Joel Talley.
Married 18 December by the Rev. Aaron Brown, Methodist. p 130

23 December 1801. William ROSE and Elizabeth Meredith, dau. David and
Elizabeth Meredith. Sur. Henry Davis. Wit. John Rose. Married
by the Rev. Aaron Brown, Methodist. p 131

15 December 1807. Daniel ROSS and Betsy Wyche. Sur. Edward Thrower.
Wit. John Wyche. Married 16 December by the Rev. Edward Dromgoole.
p 165

3 November 1778. David ROSSER and Betty Rieves, consent of Benjamin
Rieves who is surety. Wit. Benjamin Rieves, Jr. and Mary Rieves. p 20

19 October 1786. Peter ROUSE and Sarah Lawrence, dau. Robert Lawrence, deceased. Sur. Woody Lawrence. Married by the Rev. Thomas Lundie, Rector of St. Andrew's Parish. p 41

25 July 1758. Edward ROWELL and Betty Shelton, under 21, ward of Edward Rowell. Sur. Thomas Simmons. p 4

6 September 1751. Robert RUFFIN and Mary Lightfoot, widow. Sur. Lewis Parham. Robert Ruffin of Surry County. Wit. Litt. Tazewell. p 1

16 June 1787. John RUSSEL and Phebe Hudson. Married by the Rev. John King, Baptist. Ministers' Returns p 253

11 January 1803. Henry RUSSELL and Lucretia Laffoon, of age, dau. of Mary Laffoon. Sur. Isaac Russell. Married 14 January by the Rev. Aaron Brown, Methodist. p 139

12 July 1750. John RUSSELL and Sarah Edmondson. Sur. Thomas Twitty. Wit. William Clack. p 4

25 December 1804. Mathew RUSSELL and Nancy Barnes, 21. Sur. Wyatt Denton. p 149

26 May 1794. Edward F. SADLER and Mary Rose. Sur. Washington Craft. Married 29 May by the Rev. Aaron Brown, Methodist. p 81

26 January 1807. Henry SADLER and Polly Vaughan. Married 29 January by the Rev. Aaron Brown, Methodist. p 160

24 February 1800. John SADLER and Betsey Williams, 21. Sur. Thomas Anderton. Married 26 February by the Rev. Aaron Brown, Methodist. p 119

July 1787 - July 1788. Charles SALLARD and Rebecca Tucker. Married by the Rev. Thomas Lundie, Rector of St. Andrew's Parish. Ministers' Returns p 352

31 May 1798. James SAMFORD and Patsey Johnson, 21. Sur. Joseph Samford. Wit. John Williams, Green Jackson and John Johnson. Married 2 June by the Rev. Aaron Brown, Methodist. p 105

28 April 1787. Joseph SAMFORD and Milly Burks, dau. George Burks. Sur. John Minor. Wit. George BUrks, Jr. Married in May 1787 by the Rev. Thomas Lundie, Rector of St. Andrew's Parish. p 44

12 July 1791. James SANFORD and Ellen Johnson, dau. John Johnson who is surety. Married 14 July by the Rev. Aaron Brown, Methodist. p 65

26 December 1785. John SAUNDERS and Peggy Penticost, dau. Scarbrough Penticost. Sur. John Williams. Wit. John Penticost and John Harwell. p 37

23 February 1801. John SAUNDERS and Susan Williams, 21. Sur. John Phipps. Married by the Rev. Ira Ellis. p 126

18 March 1805. John SAUNDERS and Dolly W. Ezell, dau. Buckner Ezell. Sur. John Feagins. p 150

4 December 1795. Joseph SAUNDERS and Patsey Maclin, dau. Frederick Maclin. Sur. Frederick Maclin, Jr. p 88

3 May 1798. Lewis SAUNDERS and Martha Saunders. Sur. William Gholson. Married 10 May by the Rev. Aaron Brown, Methodist. p 105

22 July 1799. Turner SAUNDERS and Frances Dunn, dau. Ishmael Dunn. Sur. William Gholson. Wit. Dudley Dunn and John Greene. Married 25 July by the Rev. Aaron Brown, Methodist. p 113

23 May 1808. William SAUNDERS and Patsey Lane. Sur. Randolph Price. Wit. Jesse Coe and William Butler. p 167

23 October 1798. Enos SCARBROUGH and Nancy Neal, 21, dau. John Neal, deceased. Susanna Neal makes affidavit as to her age. Sur. Herbert Hill. Wit. Thomas Neal and Elizabeth Neal. Married 24 October by the Rev. Aaron Brown, Methodist. p 107

- February 1787. James SCARBOROUGH and Sally Saunders. Married by the Rev. Thomas Lundie, Rector of St. Andrew's Parish. Ministers' Returns p 350

15 September 1800. Sterling SCARBROUGH and Mary Reese, dau. Isham Reese. Sur. Joseph Reese. Married 19 September by the Rev. John Neblett. p 123

13 January 1798. William SCARBROUGH and Elizabeth Samford. Sur. Robert Blackwell. Wit. Sterling Scarbrough. Married by the Rev. John Neblett. p 103

29 February 1788. Gardner SCOGGINS and Martha Lucy, dau. Robert Lucy. Sur. Robert Dunkley. Married by the Rev. Thomas Lundie, Rector of St. Andrew's Parish. p 49

26 January 1809. Henry SCOGGINS and Loesa Brown. Sur. Thomas Marks. Wit. Aaron Brown. p 170

18 December 1798. John SCOGGIN and Nancy Abernathy. Sur. Frederick Abernathy. Married 20 December by the Rev. Peter Wynne. p 109

10 December 1796. William SCOGGINS and Polly Crook. Sur. Jiles Crook. Wit. John Scoggin. Married 14 December by the Rev. Henry Merritt. p 93

17 May 1808. Henry Embry SCOTT and Sarah Edmunds, dau. Thomas Edmunds. Sur. Henry Edmunds. p 167

13 April 1809. William SCOTT and Mary Davis. Married by the Rev. Peter Wynne. Ministers' Returns p 389

9 November 1795. John SEDBERRY and Polly Davis, 21. Sur. Trifard Harvey. Wit. George H. Jones. Married 12 November by the Rev. Aaron Brown, Methodist, who says Satsbury. p 87

10 October 1782. Benjamin SEWARD and Rebecca Sims. Married by the
Rev. John King, Baptist. Returned 17 January 1783. Ministers'
Returns p 345

24 December 1804. John SEWARD and Nancy Taylor. Sur. Lewis Johnson.
p 149

27 July 1807. John SEWARD and Lucy Thrower. Sur. Green Hill. p 162

12 September 1782. Joseph SEWARD and Susannah Phillips. Married by
the Rev. John King, Baptist. Returned 17 January 1783. Ministers'
Returns p 345

15 November 1802. William SEWARD and Frankey Thrower, consent of
Christopher Thrower. Sur. Green Hill. Wit. John Seward, Jr.,
and John Seward. p 136

Returned 4 February 1790. Benager SEXTON and Patsey Abernathy.
Married by the Rev. John King, Baptist. Ministers' Returns p 357

14 December 1808. William SEYMORE and Lucy Rose. Sur. Hugh M. Rose.
p 169

12 December 1803. William S. SHADBORNE and Sarah Barker, consent of
Burwell Barker. Sur. Lewis H. Linch. Married 14 December by the
Rev. Edward Dromgoole. p 143

9 December 1795. Edmunds SHELL and Patsey Lane, 21, dau. Benjamin
Lane. Sur. James HALDANE. Wit. John Shell. Married 16 December
by the Rev. Aaron Brown, Methodist, who says Edmond. p 89

- June 1786. John SHELL and Lizy Malone. Married by the Rev. Thomas
Lundie, Rector of St. Andrew's Parish. Ministers' Returns p 348

17 February 1795. John SHELL and Betsy Turner. Sur. Edmund Shell.
Wit. Thomas Gary. Married 19 February by the Rev. Aaron Brown,
Methodist. p 85

16 March 1795. Daniel SHELTON and Charlotte STAINBACK, consent of
William Stainback. Sur. Robert Watson. Wit. William Shelton and
Henry Stainback. Married by the Rev. Aaron Brown, Methodist. p 85

12 February 1800. Anderson SHORT and Mabel Short, 21. Sur. John
Cheley. Wit. Wiley Short and John Short. Married 20 February by
the Rev. Aaron Brown, Methodist. p 119

31 October 1798. Benjamin SHORT and Frances Howze, 21. Sur. Merritt
Howze. Married 11 November by the Rev. Aaron Brown, Methodist, who
says Frances House. p 107

26 November 1804. Edmund SHORT and Nancy Lanier. Sur. John Lanier.
Married 5 December by the Rev. Peter Wynne. p 148

17 December 1805. Griffin SHORT and Rebecca Short, 21. Sur. Armistead
Short. Married 19 December by the Rev. Peter Wynne. p 154

28 September 1807. Major SHORT and Polly Adams. Sur. William Rideout.
p 163

July 1787 - July 1788. William SHORT and Polly Birch. Married by the
Rev. Thomas Lundie, Rector of St. Andrew's Parish. Ministers'
Returns p 352

27 December 1802. Willie (or Wiley) SHORT and Frances T. Harrison,
consent of Cuddy Harrison. Sur. Miles King. Brunswick says Frances
F. Returned 13 January 1803 by the Rev. Wright Tucker, Episcopal
Rector. p 136

24 November 1806. Millenton SIMMS and Elizabeth Thrower. Sur. Green
Hill. p 158

29 January 1772. Benjamin SIMMONS and Sarah Butts, dau. John Butts.
Sur. Frances Young. Wit. Elizabeth Young. p 11

24 December 1773. Benjamin SIMMONS and Martha Embrey. Sur. Peter
Pelham, Jr. p 14

16 November 1796. Herbert SIMS and Nancy Wade, 21. Sur. Thomas Wade.
Wit. Peter Going and Buckner Harwell. p 92

28 November 1785. Howell SIMS and Lucy George, dau. Enoch George
who is surety. p 36

11 July 1799. Howell SIMS and Delphia Rogers, dau. John Rogers. Sur.
Reuben Rogers. p 113

6 March 1799. Richard SIMS and Rebecca Dromgoole. Sur. Swepson Sims.
Married by the Rev. Ira Ellis. p 112

24 April 1770. William SIMS and Elizabeth Wall, born 6 February 1747/8.
Sur. Drury Collier. Wit. Benjamin Chapman, Michale Wall and Rebecca
Wall. p 8

3 January 1787. James SINGLETON and Patsey Bailey. Sur. James Thompson. Married by the Rev. John King, Baptist. p 43

26 November 1792. Randle SLATE and Amy King. Sur. Isham King. Wit.
Robert Owen. p 72

26 November 1792. Randolph SLATE and Amy King. This is an error; the
original bond says Randle Slate. See Randle Slate. Brunswick p 168

9 November 1785. Robert SLATE and Salley Turner, dau. John Turner.
Sur. Lewis Brown. p 36

24 July 1786. Abraham SMITH and Lucy RAINES, dau. James Raines. Sur.
Joshua Lucy. Married by the Rev. Thomas Lundie, Rector of St.
Andrew's Parish. p 39

25 October 1773. Benjamin SMITH and Nancy Burch, dau. Richard Burch who consents. Sur. Signal Abernathy. Wit. Thomas Parham and Daniel Call. p 13

26 April 1802. Benjamin SMITH and Martha Fort. Sur. James Smith. Married 11 May by the Rev. Aaron Brown, Methodist. p 133

12 December 1800. Bolling SMITH and Lovey Owens, dau. William Owens. Sur. Berryman Ezell. Wit. William Owens, Jr. Married 18 December by the Rev. Edward Dromgoole. p 124

24 October 1802. Clement SMITH and Patsy Slate, dau. John and Polly Slate. Sur. Eli Smith. Married 27 October by the Rev. Ira Ellis. p 136

25 July 1758. Cuthbert SMITH and Elizabeth Lanier, widow. Sur. Robert Gee. p 4

21 October 1807. Cuthbert SMITH and Joanna D. Neal. Sur. Green Hill. Wit. Gabriel Smith. Married 11 November by the Rev. Aaron Brown, Methodist. p 163

27 November 1809. David SMITH and Rebecca Bass, dau. James Bass. Sur. John Pettway. p 173

22 May 1780. Eads SMITH and Mary Davis, widow. Sur. John Morris. She consents in writing. p 24

July 1787 - July 1788. Edward SMITH and Anne Fisher. Married by the Rev. Thomas Lundie, Rector of St. Andrew's Parish. Ministers' Returns p 352

15 November 1787. Frederick SMITH and Mary Broadnax. Sur. Henry Jackson. Married by the Rev. Thomas Lundie, Rector of St. Andrew's Parish. p 47

2 January 1804. Frederick SMITH and Nancy Sims, consent of Howel Sims. Sur. Samuel Roberts. Wit. Simon Lafoon and Daniel Lafoon. p 145

26 November 1810. Gabriel SMITH and Polly Banks. Sur. Thomas Parham. Married 29 November by the Rev. Cary James, Methodist, who says Mary Banks. p 177

13 July 1807. George SMITH and Caroline Hunnicut, dau. Benjamin Hunnicut. p 162

8 June 1790. James SMITH and Nancy Gargus. Caleb and Joel Manning make affidavit as to her age. Sur. Hamblin Freeman. Wit. Nicholas Falstaff. Married 10 June by the Rev. Edward Dromgoole. p 60

11 June 1796. James SMITH and Lucy Fort, ward of Isham Smith who consents. Sur. Edwin Fort. Wit. Arthur Fort. Married 13 June by the Rev. Aaron Brown, Methodist. p 91

24 November 1794.   John SMITH and Priscilla Perry, 21.   Sur. Cary
James.   Wit. Lewis Smith.   Married 29 November by the Rev. Edward
Dromgoole.   p 83

24 January 1803.   John SMITH and Ritter Nanney, 21.   Sur. Buckner
Landier.   Married 27 January by the Rev. Ira Ellis.   p 139

5 October 1804.   John SMITH and Sally Walton, 21.   Sur. Thomas Williams.
Married 12 October by the Rev. Edward Dromgoole.   p 147

4 February 1806.   John B. SMITH and Leticia Keatts, sister of H.(enry?)
Keatts.   Sur. Christopher Jones.   Married 8 February by the Rev.
Aaron Brown, Methodist.   p 155

11 December 1798.   Lewis SMITH and Sally Capel, 21.   Sur. Matthew
Newell.   Married 12 December by the Rev. Balaam Ezell, Baptist.
p 108

17 October 1791.   Millington SMITH and Betsey Mathis, dau. Lucy Mathis.
Sur. Daniel Baugh.   Wit. James Baugh.   Brunswick says Mathews. p 66

2 January 1799.   Pleasant SMITH and Polly Thompson, 21.   Sur. William
Carpenter.   Wit. David Kelly and Lemuel Ballentine.   Married 8
January by the Rev. Edward Dromgoole.   p 110

25 May 1778.   Stephen SMITH and Olive Harrison, dau. Nathaniel Harrison.
Sur. Cuddy Harrison.   Wit. Gabriel Harrison.   p 19

27 February 1809.   Sterling W. SMITH and Nancy Hartwell, over 21.   Sur.
John Harrison.   p 171

18 September 1806.   Richard S. SMITH and Frances Moore, dau. Sterling
Moore.   Sur. Richard Blalock.   Married 8 October by the Rev.
Edward Dromgoole.   p 157

25 July 1803.   William SMITH and Betsey Williams.   Sur. China Williams.
Married by the Rev. Aaron Brown, Methodist who says Elizabeth. p 141

1 April 1807.   William SMITH and Betsey Steagall.   Married by the Rev.
Aaron Brown, Methodist.   Ministers' Returns p 387

17 December 1809.   William SMITH and Sally Hogwood.   Sur. Randolph
Hogwood.   p 173

July 1789 - July 1790.   Williamson SMITH and Rebecca SMITH.   Married by
the Rev. Thomas Lundie, Rector of St. Andrew's Parish.   Ministers'
Returns p 356

24 January 1810.   John SNEAD and Catharine Jones.   Married by the Rev.
Peter Wynne.   Ministers' Returns p 389

27 July 1801.   James SPEERS and Rody Moseley.   Sur. Thomas Washington.
Married 30 July by the Rev. Balaam Ezell, Baptist.   See James Speed.
p 126

17 April 1801.   John SPENCER and Rebecca Stith, 21.   Sur. Henry Merritt.
p 126

12 March 1773. Robert SPENCER and Mary Charles, dau. Lewis Charles. Sur. Lewis Charles, Jr. Wit. Thomas Charles and Jeduthun Brent. p 13

July 1787 - July 1788. James SPICELY and Mary Abernathy. Married by the Rev. Thomas Lundie, Rector of St. Andrew's Parish. Ministers' Returns p 351

26 March 1810. James SPICELY and Ann King, of age. Sur. William Gee. p 175

22 December 1783. Francis STAINBACK and Sarah Hardaway. Sur. William Caudle. p 32

10 September 1785. Francis STAINBACK and Nancy Bass, dau. Thomas Bass. Sur. James McInvale. Both of St. Andrew's Parish. Married by the Rev. Thomas Lundie, Rector of St. Andrew's Parish. p 36

14 December 1795. James STAINBACK and Elizabeth Duggar, consent of Daniel Duggar. Sur. Richmond Duggar. Wit. Henry Morris, Sr. Married 16 December by the Rev. Aaron Brown, Methodist. p 89

20 December 1785. John STAINBACK and Mary Powell, dau. John Powell. Sur. Randolph Mitchell. Wit. John Sims, Jr. Of Meherrin Parish. Married by the Rev. Thomas Lundie, Rector of St. Andrew's Parish. p 37

24 February 1792. Robinson STAINBACK and Jincy Davenport, dau. Mary Davenport. Sur. John Owen. Wit. Polly Davenport. Married 28 February by the Rev. Aaron Brown, Methodist, who says Robertson Stainback. p 69

2 July 1793. Robert STAMPER and Keziah Bagwell. Sur. Moses Smith Hampton. Wit. Drury Bagwell. p 76

25 January 1796. James STANDLEY and Sally Ezell. Sur. Benjamin Ezell. Married 28 January by the Rev. Aaron Brown, Methodist. p 90

25 November 1800. George Steagall and Catherine Atkins, 21. Sur. William Steagall. Married 27 November by the Rev. Aaron Brown, Methodist. p 123

14 December 1786. John STEAGALL and Susanna Bedingfield. Married by the Rev. John King, Baptist. Ministers' Returns p 348

15 October 1800. Jeduthan STEED and Elizabeth Huff, 21. Sur. William Huff. Wit. Harrison Barner. Married 22 October by the Rev. James Meacham. p 123

15 October 1800. Jonathan STEED and Elizabeth Huff, 21. This is an error; original bond says Jeduthan Steed. See Jeduthan Steed. Brunswick p 172

16 February 1788. James STEWARD and Kitty Chavous. Married by the Rev. John King, Baptist. Ministers' Returns p 253

10 October 1806. Armistead STEWART and Flora Crook, dau. Betsy Crook.
Sur. Robert Crook. Armistead Stewart of Dinwiddie County. p 157

17 April 1804. Richard STEWART and Charlotte James, dau. Bob James.
Sur. Britain Grain. Married 21 April by the Rev. Ira Ellis. p 146

20 May 1807. Andrew STITH and Mary Matthews, dau. John Matthews. Sur.
Henry Stith. Wit. Bransom Dunnington and Polly Quarles. p 162

- February 1786. Buckner STITH and Elizabeth Jones. Married by the
Rev. Thomas Lundie, Rector of St. Andrew's Parish. Ministers'
Returns p 348

July 1787 - July 1788. Buckner STITH, Jr. and Nancy Walker. Married
by the Rev. Thomas Lundie, Rector of St. Andrew's Parish. Ministers'
Returns p 351

22 September 1788. Drury STITH and Fanny Love, dau. Allen Love,
deceased. Sur. Thomas Stith. Married by the Rev. Thomas Lundie,
Rector of St. Andrew's Parish. p 51

9 August 1809. Henry STITH and Mary N. Spain, dau. William Spain. Sur.
George Hardaway. Wit. Ezra Stith. p 172

24 June 1799. John STITH and Maria Meade. Susanna Meade Mother and
guardian. Sur. Buckner Stith. Wit. Nancy W. Meade, Burditt Ashton
and David Meade. John Stith of King George County. Married 27 June
by the Rev. Henry Merritt. p 113

2 May 1807. John STITH, Jr. and Nancy Cary. Sur. Green Hill. Married
3 May by the Rev. Aaron Brown, Methodist. p 161

15 April 1806. Obediah STITH and Mary L. Hunnicut, 21, dau. Benjamin
Hunnicut. Sur. Henry Stith. Wit. Benjamin Lanier. p 156

7 August 1780. Thomas STITH and Holly Bailey. Sur. William Raney. p 24

27 November 1786. Thomas STITH and Susanna Harris, dau. Matthew Harris
who is surety. Married by the Rev. Thomas Lundie, Rector of St.
Andrew's Parish. p 41

4 September 1756. William STITH and Katherine Stith. Sur. Drury Stith.
Wit. Nathaniel Edmunds and Litt. Tazewell. p 3

28 March 1787. Lewis STARKE and Dionysia Jones, dau. Peter Jones, Sr.
Sur. Edmond Stith. Married in April 1787 by the Rev. Thomas Lundie,
Rector of St. Andrew's Parish. Mentioned in her father's will pro.
26   June 1795. p 44

24 August 1756. Silvanus STOKES, Jr. and Temperance Clarke, dau. George
Clarke. Sur. Littleton Tazewell. Wit. Nicholas Edmunds. p 3

10 January 1805. Dr. William STOKES and Polly Harrison, dau. John
Harrison. Sur. Joseph Harrison. p 150

27 January 1803. Jathan STONE and Sally Dickson, of age. Sur. William Trotter. Wit. James Trotter. p 139

19 October 1806. Jathan STONE and Nancy Dixon, 21. Sur. Isaac Oldham. Married 20 November by the Rev. Peter Wynne. p 157

11 August 1807. John STONE and Vicey Sammons. Sur. Laban Pitillo. Married 15 August by the Rev. Peter Wynne who says Dicey. p 163

27 February 1801. Peter STONE and Fanny Sammons. Sur. Lebon Petillo. Wit. Luis Lambert. Margaret Stone consents for Peter Stone. Married by the Rev. Peter Wynne. p 126

22 March 1784. Richard STONE and Delitha Gibs. Sur. William Gibs. p 32

29 November 1752. James STUART and Elizabeth Irby. Sur. John Irby. p 1

5 April 1793. John STURDIVANT and Susanna Collier, dau. Charles Collier, Sr. Sur. James Hicks, Jr. Wit. Charles Collier, Jr. Married 6 April by the Rev. John Loyd. p 75

16 December 1802. William STURDIVANT and Martha Cheely, dau. Joseph Cheely. Sur. John Lewis. Wit. John Judd. Married 23 December by the Rev. Peter Wynne. p 137

7 January 1798. Benjamin SUGGETT and Nancy Sturdivant, dau. John Sturdivant. Sur. Herbert Hill. Wit. Jesse Sturdivant and Lucas Sturdivant. p 103

23 July 1789. Edcomb SUGGITT and Molly Jones, 21, dau. Stephen Jones. Sur. John Jones. Wit. Sarah Jones. Edcomb Suggitt of Mecklenburg County. p 55

23 August 1796. Joel TALLEY and Rebecca Rose, 21. Sur. Robert Latimer. Wit. James Davis and Charles B. Jones. Married 8 September by the Rev. Aaron Brown, Methodist. p 91

2 November 1799. William TALLY and Rebecca Briggs, 21. Sur. Frederick Briggs. Wit. Samuel Scarbrough. p 115

26 January 1801. John TANSIL and Betsey Collier, 21. Sur. James Harrison. p 126

4 August 1800. Edward Jones TARPLEY and Mary Baker Manson, dau. Thomas Manson. Sur. Thomas Jones. Wit. Pascal Jones. Edward Jones Tarpley ward of Joseph Maclin. p 122

19 June 1799. Joel TARPLEY and Elizabeth Johnson, 21. Sur. John Phipps. Wit. Philip Owen. Married by the Rev. Ira Ellis. p 112

21 December 1796. John TARPLEY and Sally Barrow, dau. William Barrow who is surety. Wit. Freeman Jones. p 94

16 October 1786. Thomas TARPLEY and Milly Moore, 21. Sur. Samuel
Moore. Wit. Drury Mathis. Married by the Rev. Thomas Lundie,
Rector of St. Andrew's Parish. Brunswick says Sally Moore which
is an error; the original bond says Milly Moore. p 41

5 August 1803. Michael TARWATER and Caty Trotter, 21, dau. George
Trotter. Sur. George Trotter, Jr. Wit. James Trotter, Thomas
Trotter, Nancy Trotter and Martha Trotter. p 141

10 January 1797. Edward TATUM and Mary Ogborne, dau. James Ogburn.
Sur. William Ogborne. p 95

27 February 1797. Herbert TATUM and Eliza Ogborne. Sur. William
Ogborne. p 97

23 February 1804. John TATUM (?) and Elizabeth Moore. Married by
the Rev. Peter Wynne. Ministers' Returns p 381

28 May 1787. Jesse TATUM and Polly Cook, 21. Affidavit from James
Green and Benjamin Warren as to her age. Sur. Benjamin Warren.
Married by the Rev. John King, Baptist. p 45

13 July 1797. Osburn TATUM and Susanna Harwell, 21. Sur. Parten Bass.
Wit. George H. Jones. Married by the Rev. Hubbard Saunders. p 99

5 January 1799. Sihon TATUM and Martha Ogborne. Sur. William Ogborne.
Married 6 January by the Rev. John Neblett. p 110

24 May 1803. Benjamin TAYLOR and Nancy Williams. Sur. John Williams.
Married 26 May by the Rev. Aaron Brown, Methodist. p 141

20 December 1791. Cornelius TAYLOR and Jane Haymour. Sur. Mark
Haymour. Wit. Joseph Taylor. Cornelius Taylor son of Joseph
Taylor. Consent of John and Jeney Haymour. Married 22 December
by the Rev. Aaron Brown, Methodist. p 67

9 December 1805. Daniel TAYLOR and Cressey Waller, 21. Sur. Richard
Taylor. p 153

20 December 1758. Henry TAYLOR and Temperance Peterson, dau. John
Peterson. Sur. Archibald Wager. Wit. Betty Brown and Lucy Thorp(?).
Henry Taylor from Southampton County. p 5

6 December 1803. Jones TAYLOR and Jincy Matthews, 21. Sur. Luke
Matthews. Wit. George Hudson and P. Russell. Married by the Rev.
Aaron Brown, Methodist, who says Jean. p 143

3 August 1797. Jesse TAYLOR and Lucretia Watson. Sur. George Walton.
Wit. Littleton Walton and Edmond Lanier. Married by the Rev.
Edward Dromgoole. p 99

6 August 1790. John TAYLOR and Aylce Atkins. Sur. Jehu Atkins. Wit.
John L. Wilkins. Married 8 August by the Rev. John King, Baptist.
p 60

24 June 1800. John TAYLOR and Polly C. Perry, 21. Sur. Benjamin
Strange. Wit. Joseph Lyell. Married 27 June by the Rev. John
Neblett. p 121

24 December 1792. Lewis TAYLOR and Betsey Braswell, dau. Jesse Braswell who is surety. Returned 20 January 1793 by the Rev. John King,
Baptist. p 73

1 December 1804. Mackey TAYLOR and Sally Taylor, dau. Daniel Taylor.
Sur. Joseph Moseley. p 148

22 January 1801. Richard TAYLOR and Nancy Britt, dau. Benjamin Britt.
Sur. Allso Taylor. Wit. Henry Britt. Married by the Rev. Ira Ellis.
p 125

20 December 1801. Robert TAYLOR and Nancy Carpenter, 21. Sur. Isaac
Carpenter. Married 24 December by the Rev. Ira Ellis. p 131

12 February 1810. Robert A. TAYLOR and Margaret Saunders. Sur. Joseph
Saunders. Married 14 February by the Rev. William Dossey, Baptist.
p 174

28 April 1798. William TAYLOR and Susanna Singleton. Sur. Cornelius
Taylor. Wit. Hezekiah Singleton and Elizabeth Singleton. p 105

7 February 1801. Thomas TENSBLUM and Mary C. Holderby. See Thomas
Tinsbloom.   Brunswick p 178

18 December 1788. John THACKER and Nancy Overby. Sur. Reuel Lewis.
p 51

16 October 1806. William THACKER and Elizabeth Dunkley. Sur. Robert
Lucy. p 157

22 June 1809. Burrell THERESTA and Nancy Rawlings. Married by the
Rev. Peter Wynne. Ministers' Returns p 389

7 September 1805. Allen THOMAS and Leodicia Shell. Sur. Freeman
Shell. p 152

22 February 1794. Daniel THOMAS and Milley Singleton, 21. Sur. Henry
Singleton. Wit. John Thomas and Willie Jones. p 79

18 November 1805. David THOMAS and Patsey Moseley, 21. Sur. Willie
Harrison. p 152

14 October 1786. John THOMAS and Sarah Lawrence. Sur. Wood Lawrence.
Married by the Rev. Thomas Lundie, Rector of St. Andrew's Parish.
p 41

July 1789 - July 1790. John THOMAS and Frances Tyus. Married by the
Rev. Thomas Lundie, Rector of St. Andrew's Parish. Ministers'
Returns p 356

28 October 1789. Peter THOMAS and Hannah Wall, widow of Henry Wall. Sur. Thomas Steagall. Wit. Samuel Jones. Married by the Rev. John King, Baptist. p 56

5 November 1791. Peter THOMAS, Jr. and Martha Wall, ward of Peter Thomas, Sr. who is surety. p 66

26 December 1803. Richard THOMAS and Noah Moseley. Sur. Nicodemus Moseley. Wit. David Thomas. Her own consent is signed Noah Moseley checked by original bond. p 144

26 December 1803. Richard THOMAS and Patsy Moseley, widow. I think this is an error and is intended for the above bond. Brunswick p 178

16 December 1799. Bannister THOMASON and Polly (Mary) Taylor. Sur. Abel Edmunds. Married 18 December by the Rev. John Neblett. p 116

24 May 1798. John THOMSON and Ann Turner. Married by the Rev. Aaron Brown, Methodist. Ministers' Returns p 368

11 January 1802. Darville THOMPSON and Prissey Burdge. Sur. Frederick Burdge. p 132

22 December 1783. James THOMPSON and Sally Ball Quarles, dau. Moses Quarles, Sr. Sur. William Roper. Wit. Moses Quarles, Jr. p 32

5 March 1781. Nathaniel THOMPSON and Eliza Donaldson Dupree, dau. Thomas (?) Dupree. p 26

16 February 1774. William THORNTON and Sarah Goodrich, dau. Edward Goodrich. Sur. John Clack. p 15

24 December 1783. Randol (or Randle) THREADGILL and Susanna Smith, dau. James Smith. Sur. Thomas Threadgill. p 32

29 August 1805. John THREAT and Susanna Peebles. Ministers' Returns p 382

24 September 1781. Christopher THROWER and Sally Sims, dau. John Sims, deceased. Sur. William Randle. p 26

1 April 1809. Joseph THWEATT and Sally Powell. Married by the Rev. Peter Wynne. Ministers' Returns p 389

29 May 1810. Thomas THWEATT and Mary Ann Coleman, consent of Richard Coleman. Sur. Bradford Burge. Married 30 May by the Rev. Peter Wynne. p 176

Returned 4 February 1790. Michael TILLEY and Sarah Mize. Married by the Rev. John King, Baptist. Ministers' Returns p 357

9 December 1799. Blumer TILLMAN and Sally High, dau. David High. Sur. Philip Huff. p 116

28 August 1797. Jarratt TILLMAN and Lucretia Fann, 21. Sur. John White. Married 30 August by the Rev. John Loyd. p 99

27 August 1810. John TILLMAN and Salley Ryland. Sur. Edward B. Ryland. Married 30 August by the Rev. Cary James, Methodist. p 176

- - 1789. Roger TILLMAN and Tabitha Turner. Married by the Rev. John King, Baptist. Ministers' Returns p 354

30 August 1797. Jarratt TILMAN and Lucretia Funn. Married by the Rev. John Loyd. Ministers' Returns p 367

23 May 1758. John TILMAN and Mary Simmons. Sur. John Daniel. p 4

7 February 1801. Thomas TINSBLOOM and Mary C. Holderby. Sur. Joseph Holderby. Wit. John Maclin. See Thomas Tensblum. p 126

27 September 1779. James TOMLINSON and Elizabeth Morris,widow. Sur. William Robinson. Wit. William Sykes and Reuben Cheek. p 22

July 1788 - July 1789. John TOMLINSON and Sarah Stewart. Married by the Rev. Thomas Lundie, Rector of St. Andrew's Parish. Ministers' Returns p 354

27 April 1792. Joseph TRAYLOR and Mary Jackson, 21. Sur. Peter Wynne. Wit. William Williams and David Roper. Married by the Rev. Thomas Lundie, Rector of St. Andrew's Parish. p 70

26 January 1799. Peter TRAYLOR and Selah Rainey. Married by the Rev. Peter Wynne. Ministers' Returns p 370

18 December 1800. Peter TRAYLOR and Amey Ross. Married by the Rev. Peter Wynne. Ministers' Returns p 376

6 December 1799. Thomas TRICE and Sarah Hill. Sur. Burwell Lanier. p 116

9 November 1802. Benjamin TROTTER and Mary S. Brown. Sur. Aaron Brown. p 136

16 December 1772. George TROTTER and Caty Crook. Sur. James Trotter. Wit. Peter Jones and Isham Smith. p 12

27 October 1804. George TROTTER and Mary B. Hightower. Sur. William Trotter. Married 1 November by the Rev. Aaron Brown, Methodist. p 147

22 November 1773. Isham TROTTER and Jenny Burch, dau. Richard Burch. Sur. William Lanier. Wit. Thomas Parham and George Trotter. p 14

27 May 1795. Isham TROTTER and Elizabeth Whitehead, dau. Benjamin Whitehead. Sur. John Richardson. Wit. Robert Winn, John Richardson and Angilico Whitehead. Married by the Rev. John Neblett. p 86

13 September 1781. James TROTTER, Sr., and Hannah Wilson. Sur. Isham Trotter. p 26

28 April 1795. James TROTTER and Catey Keatts, dau. James Keatts.
Sur. Henry Keatts. Wit. William Trotter and Frances Keatts. p 85

10 January 1801. James TROTTER and Eleznor Rose. Sur. William
Trotter. Married 12 January by the Rev. Aaron Brown, Methodist.
p 125

27 January 1803. James TROTTER and Lucy Pritchett, under age, dau.
Joshua Pritchett. Sur. William Trotter. p 139

27 October 1794. Richard TROTTER and Elizabeth Trotter. Sur. George
Trotter. p 82

11 March 1799. Thomas TROTTER and Polly S. Quarles. Sur. Moses
Quarles, Jr. Married 14 March by the Rev. Peter Wynne who says
Mary Quarles. p 112

6 September 1799. William TROTTER and Lucy Fowlkes, dau. Thomas
Fowlkes. Sur. William S. Collier. Married 12 September by the
Rev. Aaron Brown, Methodist. p 114

July 1790 - July 1791. David TUCKER and Judith Harper. Married by
the Rev. Thomas Lundie, Rector of St. Andrew's Parish. Ministers'
Returns p 359

21 December 1786. Frederick TUCKER and Polly Crowder. Sur. Ephraim
Jackson. Married by the Rev. John King, Baptist. p 42

7 January 1804. Sterling TUCKER and Mary Ann Ingram. Sur. Hartwell
Tucker. Married 12 January by the Rev. Wright Tucker, Episcopal
Rector. p 145

5 March 1784. Wright TUCKER and Elizabeth Williamson, dau. Charles
Williamson. Sur. Heartwell Tucker. Wit. Sterling Tucker. p 32

- - 1787. John TUDOR and Milley Spurlock. Married by the Rev.
John King, Baptist. Ministers' Returns p 253

28 November 1796. Littleberry TURBEFIELD and Martha Connelly, of age.
Sur. Seth Turbefield. Wit. William Raney. Returned 22 December by
the Rev. Peter Wynne. p 93

8 April 1784. Seth TURBYFILL and Dolly King, dau. Charles King. Sur.
David Fowler. p 33

14 December 1785. William TURBYFILL and Rebecca Scarbrough, dau. John
Scarbrough. Sur. Henry Andrews. Of St. Andrew's Parish. Married
by the Rev. Thomas Lundie. p 36

23 November 1801. Robert TRUNBULL, Jr., and Elizabeth I. Stith. Sur.
David Robinson. Wit. Herbert Hill. p 129

19 April 1791. Benjamin TURNER and Elizabeth Clack, 21. Sur. James
Clack. Wit. Anges B. Clack. Married 23 April by the Rev. Aaron
Brown, Methodist. p 65

7 February 1784. Jesse TURNER and Anne Meredith. Sur. Thomas Stone.
p 32

13 February 1797. Matthew TURNER, Jr., and Wilmuth Malone, 21. Sur.
John Malone. Wit. George Malone and Mills Malone. p 96

26 December 1805. John USSERY and Mary J. Brown. Married by the Rev.
Peter Wynne. Ministers' Returns p 382

29 November 1804. Samuel USSERY and Matilda Ussery. Married by the
Rev. Peter Wynne. Ministers' Returns p 382

9 May 1805. Binns VAUGHAN and Nancy Williams, 21. Sur. John H.
Vaughan. Married 10 May by the Rev. Aaron Brown, Methodist. p 151

17 October 1781. David VAUGHAN and Hannah Hightower, widow. Sur.
Richard Vaughan. p 26

21 December 1785. Harrod VAUGHAN and Dicey McKenny. Sur. John
Durkley. Of St. Andrew's Parish. Married by the Rev. Thomas
Lundie who says Herod Vaughan. p 37

27 October 1783. James VAUGHAN and Mary (or Martha) Malone, dau.
George Malone. Sur. Howard Bailey. p 31

26 March 1804. James VAUGHAN and Polly Bass. Sur. Benjamin Bass.
Married 19 March by the Rev. Hubbard Saunders. p 146

3 January 1807. James VAUGHAN and Susanna Garrett. Sur. Henry Sadler.
Married 8 Janaury by the Rev. Aaron Brown, Methodist. p 160

21 September 1791. Jeremiah VAUGHAN and Martha Steagall, dau. Thomas
Steagall who is surety. Married by the Rev. John King, Baptist. p 66

9 January 1804. John High VAUGHAN and Rebecca Drake. Sur. Thomas
Drake. Married 10 January by the Rev. Hubbard Saunders. p 145

9 May 1810. John VAUGHAN and Polly Bentley. Married by the Rev.
Peter Wynne. Ministers' Returns p 389

24 December 1804. Lewiston H. VAUGHAN and Sally Allen. Sur. Howard
Allen. p 149

10 October 1791. Micajah VAUGHAN and Delilah McKenney. Sur. William
McKenney. Married by the Rev. Thomas Lundie, Rector of St.
Andrew's Parish. p 66

11 July 1800. Moody VAUGHAN and Polly Lett, 21. Sur. George Vaughan.
Wit. James Vaughan. Married 12 July by the Rev. Hubbard Saunders.
p 121

16 November 1801. Richard VAUGHAN and Tabitha Edwards, dau. Jesse
Edwards. Sur. Jordan Edwards. Wit. Clement Hancocke. Married
by the Rev. Ira Ellis who says Patsey Edwards. p 129

26 June 1797. Stephen VAUGHAN and Lucy Rideout. Giles Rideout makes affidavit as to her age. Sur. Arthur Fort. Wit. Edwing Fort. Brunswick says _Suky_ which is an error; original bond says Lucy Rideout. p 99

24 November 1795. William VAUGHAN and Patsey Berry, 21. Sur. William Meredith. Wit. Philip Claiborne, Henry Watson and Meredith Moss. Married by the Rev. Aaron Brown, Methodist. p 88

26 July 1802. William VAUGHAN and Tempe Emmery, 21. Sur. Stephen Vaughan. p 134

20 June 1806. Capt. William VAUGHAN and Peggy Rice, 21. Sur. Herbert Hill. Wit. William Rice. Married 21 June by the Rev. William Dossey, Baptist. p 156

22 April 1793. William VICK and Elizabeth Powell, 21. Sur. John Stainback. Wit. Thomas Lundie. Married by the Rev. Aaron Brown, Methodist. p 75

31 January 1799. David WADE and Betsey Williams, dau. Alexander Williams. Sur. Thomas Wade. Returned 17 February by the Rev. Balaam Ezell, Baptist who says _Elizabeth_. p 111

- August 1785. Samuel WAINWRIGHT and Nancy Thomas of Bath Parish. Married by the Rev. Thomas Lundie, Rector of St. Andrew's Parish. Ministers' Returns p 345

20 February 1787. Alexander WALKER and Sarah Elliott, dau. Richard Elliott. Sur. William Elliott. Married by the Rev. Thomas Lundie, Rector of St. Andrew's Parish. p 43

31 May 1786. David WALKER and Mary Elliott. Sur. Richard Elliott. Wit. Edmund Stith. Married by the Rev. Thomas Lundie, Rector of St. Andrew's Parish. p 39

15 December 1806. David WALKER and Elizabeth Hardaway. Sur. George Hardaway. p 159

Returned 4 February 1790. George WALKER and Phebe Cheatham. Married by the Rev. John King, Baptist. Ministers' Returns p 357

19 December 1785. Henry WALKER and Martha Winfield. Sur. Edward Walker. Of Meherrin Parish. Married by the Rev. Thomas Lundie, Rector of St. Andrew's Parish. p 37

18 May 1805. Jesse WALKER and Dicey Wesson, 21. Sur. Anderson Wesson. Married 23 May by the Rev. Hubbard Saunders. p 151

26 November 1772. William WALKER and Ann Harrison. Sur. Benjamin Harrison. p 12

21 December 1789. William WALKER and Agnes Birchett. Sur. Edward Walker. Wit. Edward Birchett and Theodoric Birchett. Married by the Rev. Thomas Lundie, Rector of St. Andrew's Parish. p 57

21 November 1797. William WALKER and Nancy V. Hicks. Sur. Edward Walker. Wit. William Walker. p 100

25 October 1784. Wilson WALKER and Anglica Mathis, consent of Luke Mathis. Sur. Mark Steed. Brunswick says Mathews. p 33

28 January 1795. George WALL and Martha House, 21. Mary House makes affidavit as to her age. Sur. Henry Wall. Wit. Frances House and Marritt House. p 34

22 June 1807. John WALL and Levina Cole. Sur. William Edward Broadnax. Frederick Smith. Married 27 June by the Rev. Aaron Brown, Methodist. p 162

2 November 1808. John WALL and Lucretia Mize, 21. Sur. John Mize. p 168

19 December 1787. Peter WALL and Mary Mize. Married by the Rev. John King, Baptist. Ministers' Returns p 253

6 September 1797. Jesse WALLACE and Faithy Walpole. Sur. William Walpole. Married 7 September by the Rev. Aaron Brown, Methodist. p 99

1 September 1796. Starling WALLER and Rebecca Drumright. Married by the Rev. Peter Wynne. Ministers' Returns p 366

4 January 1798. Robert WALLOC (?) and Nancy Moore. Married by the Rev. Peter Wynne. Ministers' Returns p 368

21 November 1805. Benjamin WALPOLE and Sally Johnson, consent of William M. Johnson. Sur. William Johnson. Married 4 December by the Rev. Aaron Brown, Methodist. p 152

23 December 1805. John WALPOLE and Polly James. Sur. William James. p 154

22 June 1798. Richard WALPOLE and Agnes Freeman. Sur. Hamlin Freeman. Married 4 July by the Rev. Aaron Brown, Methodist. p 106

3 October 1789. William WALPOLE and Lucy Johnson, consent of John Johnson. Sur. Thomas Goodrum. William Walpole, 21, son of Thomas Walpole. Married by the Rev. Aaron Brown, Methodist. p 55

27 September 1785. Drury WALTON and Gracy Ingram, dau. Joseph Ingram, who is surety. p 36

26 January 1789. Elias Rowe WALTON and Mary Britt. Sur. Henry Britt. p 53

20 December 1787. Isaac WALTON and Elizabeth Allen. Married by the Rev. John King, Baptist. Ministers' Return p 253

13 March 1797. John WALTON and Polly Warwick, 21. Sur. George Johnson. Wit. Jesse Taylor and John Goodrich. Married 16 March by the Rev. Edward Dromgoole. p 97

23 April 1806. Joshua WALTON and Susannah Elizabeth Hicks, dau. James Hicks. Sur. Joseph Harrison. Wit. Harrison Hartwell. p 156

1 August 1786. Thomas WALTON and Mary Skinner, over 21. Sur. Henry Walton. Wit. William Allen and Mary Allen. Married by the Rev. John King, Baptist. p 40

24 September 1798. Thomas WALTON and Elizabeth Porch, dau. Thomas Porch (or Poarch). Sur. John Walton. p 107

11 December 1802. William WALTON and Lucy Britt, dau. Benjamin Britt. Sur. Elias R. Walton. Wit. Ira Ellis. Married 14 December by the Rev. Ira Ellis. p 137

25 September 1786. Richard WARD and Winny Smith, dau. James Smith. Sur. William Ward. Married by the Rev. Thomas Lundie, Rector of St. Andrew's Parish. p 40

23 December 1793. Willie WARD and Middy Smith, 21. Stephen Gibbs makes affidavit as to her age. Sur. Cary James. Wit. Thomas Lanier. Married 26 December by the Rev. Edward Dromgoole. p 78

27 January 1784. James WARDEN and Lucy Hall. This is an error; original bond says James Warsden. See James Warsden. Brunsick p 190

27 July 1778. Benjamin WARREN and Tempe Bass. Sur. John Jeter. p 19

19 December 1791. Wiley Prince WARREN and Elizabeth Payne. Sur. John Johnson. Wit. Col. John Jones and James Samford. p 67

20 December 1791. William P. WARREN and Elizabeth Payne. Married by the Rev. Aaron Brown, Methodist. Ministers' Returns p 359

27 January 1784. James WARSDEN and Lucy Hall. Sur. Briggs Goodrich. p 32

- December 1787. John Henry WARTMAN and Tabitha Epps. Married by the Rev. John King, Baptist. Ministers' Returns p 253

12 December 1808. William WARWICK and Margaret Seward. Sur. William Seward. p 169

25 December 1791. Gray WASHINGTON and Nancy Harrison, dau. James Harrison. Sur. Willie Harrison. Wit. Gronow Owen. Married by the Rev. Thomas Lundie, Rector of St. Andrew's Parish. p 67

22 November 1784. Thomas WASHINGTON and Janet Love, dau. Allan Love. Sur. Henry Walker. Wit. Wilson Walker. p 34

29 January 1805. Warner WASHINGTON and Arianna Stith. Sur. Lawrence W. Stith. Warner Washington of King George County. p 150

8 August 1809. Frederick WATKINS and Christianna Gresham. Sur. Gregory Gresham. p 172

6 May 1794. Henry A. WATKINS and Ann Edmunds. Sur. John Orgain.
Brunswick says Henry W. p 81

19 December 1789. John WATSON and Lucy Watson. Sur. George Watson.
Wit. John Jones and Hamlin Freeman. Brunswick says Lucretia Walton.
Married by the Rev. Edward Dromgoole. p 56

13 August 1798. Henry WATSON and Rebecca Butler. Brunswick p 192

29 August 1783. Septimus WEATHERBY and Sarah Myrick, dau. John Myrick,
Sr. Sur. John Myrick, Jr. p 31

18 December 1779. William WEAVER and Rebecca Whittington. Sur. John
Whittington. p 23

26 December 1808. Edmund WEBB and Nancy Floyd. Sur. Charles Floyd.
p 169

26 November 1798. James WEBB and Rebecca Pearson, 21. Sur. Isaac
Ledbetter. Wit. Harbert Alley. Returned 10 January 1799 by the Rev.
Edward Dromgoole. p 108

22 August 1803. James WEBB and Frances Hicks, 21. Sur. Samuel Bracey.
Married 8 September by the Rev. Edward Dromgoole. p 141

27 February 1804. Joseph WELLS and Sally Thrift. Married by the Rev.
Peter Wynne. Ministers' Returns p 382

16 July 1800. Thomas WELLS and Salley Lanier. Sur. Benjamin Bass.
p 122

- November 1785. William WELLS and Sarah Westmoreland of Bath Parish.
Married by the Rev. Thomas Lundie, Rector of St. Andrew's Parish.
Ministers' Returns p 345

24 August 1801. William WELLS and Sally Gee, dau. Robert Gee. Sur.
Absalom Harwell. Married 2 September by the Rev. Peter Wynne. p 128

3 October 1782. - WESSON and Sally Nanney. Married by the Rev. John
King, Baptist. Returned 17 January 1783. Ministers' Returns p 345

4 December 1806. Anderson WESSON and Jincey Mason (or Wesson). Sur.
Joseph R. Walker. p 159

4 December 1799. Buckner WESSON and Nancy House, 21. Sur. Absalom
Williams. Wit. John Braswell. Married 6 December by the Rev.
Balaam Ezell, Baptist. p 116

26 December 1785. Edward WESSON and Rebecca Nanny. Sur. Drury Nanny.
Married 29 December by the Rev. John King, Baptist. p 37

23 December 1805. Edward WESSON and Jincey Williams, dau. Mary
Williams. Sur. John House. p 154

25 December 1809. Isaac WESSON and Sabra Seward, dau. Joseph Seward.
Sur. Joseph Kelly. Wit. John Rhea. Brunswick says Tabitha. Married
26 December by the Rev. Cary James, Methodist, who says Sabra. p 173

28 January 1788. James WESSON and Nancy Clary, dau. Harrid Clary. Sur.
Reuben Wray. Wit. Benjamin Warren. Married 7 February by the
Rev. John King, Baptist. p 49

9 December 1795. John WESSON and Elizabeth Jones, consent of Jesse
Jones. Sur. Thomas Howard. Wit. John P. James, William Moore and
Hicks Jones. Married 17 December by the Rev. Edward Dromgoole. p 89

21 December 1808. John WESSON and Delilah Massey, 21. Sur. Isaac
Wesson. Married 22 December by the Rev. Edward Dromgoole. p 169

4 November 1797. Julius WESSON and Lucy Wesson. Sur. Henry Wesson.
Married 9 November by the Rev. Edward Dromgoole. p 100

23 December 1793. Littleton WESSON and Betsy Justice, 21. William
Justice makes affidavit as to her age. Sur. Thomas Wesson. Wit.
William Wesson, John Wesson, Zenas Fox & Lewis B. Taylor. Married
25 December by the Rev. Edward Dromgoole. p 78

22 December 1794. Thomas WESSON and Lucy Kelly, dau. Moses Kelly. Sur.
Littleton Wesson. Wit. William Wesson, Littleberry Wesson and Mark
Justice. Married 25 December by the Rev. Edward Dromgoole. p 83

13 November 1798. Thomas WESSON and Nancy Jones, of age. Sur. John
Wesson. Wit. Hix Jones. Married 14 November by the Rev. Balaam
Ezell, Baptist. p 108

31 March 1809. Washington WESSON and Cesley Pearson, dau. John Pearson,
deceased, ward of Morris Pearson. Sur. James Mason. Wit. William
Jones and Cannon Jones. Married by the Rev. Edward Dromgoole. p 171

16 December 1796. Wiley WESSON and Hannah Howard, ward of Francis
Smith. Sur. James Wesson. Wit. Thomas Howard and Hicks Jones.
Married by the Rev. Edward Dromgoole. See Willie Wesson. p 94

29 April 1786. William WESSON and Rebecca Roberts. Sur. Stephen Gibbs.
William Justice gives affidavit as to her age. Married 2 May by the
Rev. John King, Baptist. p 39

27 December 1791. William WESSON and Rebecca Vaughan, age 21 in March
1791, dau. James Vaughan. Sur. David Blalock. Wit. Thomas Williams.
p 68

16 December 1796. Willie WESSON and Hannah Howard. See Wiley Wesson.
Brunswick p 194

20 December 1794. Ephraim WEST and Elizabeth Ingram, 21. Sur.
Bartholomew Ingram. Wit. Willie Jones. p 83

24 February 1794. John WEST and Lucy Williams. Sur. Lewis Holloway.
Married by the Rev. Peter Wynne. p 80

25 October 1802. Jesse WESTMORELAND and Eliza G. Ingram, 21. Sur. Washington Croft. Married 14 November by the Rev. Hubbard Saunders. p 136

28 December 1801. Peterson WESTMORELAND and Eliza Jolly. Sur. Nathaniel Edwards. Wit. Thomas Lanier. Married 29 December by the Rev. Hubbard Saunders. p 131

26 March 1787. Robert WESTMORELAND and Lucy Freeman, over 21, dau. Henry Freeman, deceased. Sur. Sterling Caple. Married by the Rev. John King, Baptist. p 44

21 June 1806. Moses WHEELER and Elizabeth Carpenter, 21. Sur. George Atkins. p 156

28 January 1793. Robert L. WHITAKER and Sally Leadbetter. Sur. Henry Leadbetter. Wit. Nathaniel Lucas. Married 30 January by the Rev. Edward Dromgoole. p 74

26 December 1796. Burwell WHITBY and Molley Nanny. Sur. John Nanny. Married 29 December by the Rev. Edward Dromgoole. See Burwell Whittey. p 95

11 December 1809. Robert WHITBY and Middy Nanny. Sur. Drury Nanny. Married 14 December by the Rev. Cary James, Methodist. p 173

22 November 1796. John WHITE and Susanna Gunn. Sur. John Tillman. Married 23 November by the Rev. Aaron Brown, Methodist. p 93

15 December 1800. John WHITE and Sally Steed. Sur. Mark Steed. p 124

20 February 1800. Samuel WHITE and Nancy Barker, 21. Sur. Ezekiel Blanch. Married by the Rev. James Meacham. p 119

8 February 1803. Stephen WHITE and Mary Hearn, 21. Sur. Daniel White. p 140

26 November 1795. Valentine WHITE and Molly Cooke. Sur. Frederick Cooke. p 88

17 December 1786. William WILKERSON and Elizabeth Stainback, consent of Lucy Stainback. Sur. Robinson Stainback. p 42

26 October 1807. Robert Wilkinson and Polly Robinson. Sur. Henry Robinson. p 164

17 February 1801. Thomas WILKINSON and Biddy Browder. Sur. William Browder. p 126

6 March 1790. William WHITTEMORE and Ann Adams. Sur. Gower Addams. p 58

26 May 1806. Lewis WHITTINGTON and Frances Brown. Sur. William T. Pennington. Married by the Rev. William Dossey, Baptist. p 156

24 August 1801. John WILBORNE and Elizabeth Abernathy. Sur. William
Rainey. Returned 8 October by the Rev. Aaron Brown, Methodist.
See John Welborne. p 128

- December 1786. William WILKENSON and Elizabeth Stainback. Married
by the Rev. Thomas Lundie, Rector of St. Andrew's Parish. Ministers'
Returns p 350

26 November 1787. John WILKES and Elizabeth Steagall. Sur. George
Steagall. Married by the Rev. John King, Baptist. p 47

26 January 1795. Joseph WILKES and Polly Jackson, dau. Ephraim Jackson.
Sur. Herbert Hill. Married 29 January by the Rev. Aaron Brown,
Methodist. p 84

July 1789 - July 1790. Elisha WILKESON and Lucy Abernathy. Married by
the Rev. Thomas Lundie, Rector of St. Andrew's Parish. Ministers'
Returns p 356

20 October 1790. John L. WILKINS and Katharine Stith. Sur. William W.
Wilkins. Wit. Polly Garland and Clarissa Read. Married by the
Rev. Thomas Lundie, Rector of St. Andrew's Parish, who says
Catharine. p 61

20 September 1799. Joseph WILKINS and Elizabeth Jones. Sur. George W.
Jones. Married 21 September by the Rev. Aaron Brown, Methodist. p 114

14 May 1782. Burwell WILKS and Susanna Cordle, dau. Mary Cordle. Sur.
William Cordle. Wit. Joseph Wilks. Thomas Morris gives consent. p 28

27 January 1800. Absolem WILLIAMS and Charlotte Nanny. Sur. Amos
Nanny. Married by the Rev. Balaam Ezell, Baptist. p 119

17 March 1770. Alexander WILLIAMS and Elizabeth Sims, 21, dau. of John
Sims. Sur. William Sims. Wit. David Sims. p 8

7 January 1810. Benjamin WILLIAMS and Nancy Manly, dau. Richard Manly,
consent only. p 174

23 November 1807. Burwell WILLIAMS and Lucy Lewis. Sur. William Lewis.
p 164

21 December 1796. David WILLIAMS and Diannah Edwards, dau. Jesse
Edwards. Sur. Thomas Edwards. Wit. Herbert Edwards. Married 22
December by the Rev. Edward Dromgoole. p 94

16 January 1804. David WILLIAMS and Elizabeth Balentine. Sur. Dudley
Dunn. Wit. Nancy Hill and Patsey C. Mitchell. p 145

26 May 1806. Edmund WILLIAMS and Elizabeth Williams. Sur. John
Williams. Wit. J. P. Malone. p 156

2 June 1808. Garrett WILLIAMS and Winefred Lanier, 21. Sur. John
Williams. Wit. Ozburn Williams. p 167

24 November 1806. George WILLIAMS and Elizabeth H. Foster. Sur. John Phipps. Returned 30 December by the Rev. Hubbard Saunders. p 158

25 January 1802. Isaac WILLIAMS and Tabitha House, 21. Sur. John Phipps. p 132

6 May 1798. James WILLIAMS and Rebecca Parker. Sur. Rives Parker. Wit. Sterling Parker, William Linch and James Linch. Married 10 May by the Rev. Balaam Ezell, Baptist. p 105

22 September 1788. John WILLIAMS and Frances Strange, 21. Sur. John Moss. Wit. William HARRISON and Thomas Boswell. Married by the Rev. John King, Baptist. p 51

25 March 1805. John R. WILLIAMS and Betsey Wray. Married by the Rev. Aaron Brown, Methodist. Ministers' Returns p 386

27 March 1805. John WILLIAMS and Betsy Bass. See John R. Williamson. Brunswick p 198

16 December 1809. John WILLIAMS and Nancy Betty. Sur. William Mason. p 173

26 December 1803. John WILLIAMS and Nancy Braswell. Sur. Jesse Braswell. Married 5 January 1804 by the Rev. Hubbard Saunders. p 144

26 December 1786. Jones WILLIAMS and Elizabeth Clark, dau. Elisha Clark. Sur. Drury Stith. Jones Williams, Sr., guardian of Jones Williams. Married by the Rev. John King, Baptist. p 43

24 August 1801. Jones WILLIAMS and Elizabeth Evans, dau. Evan Evans. Sur. Peter Williams. Married 26 August by the Rev. Aaron Brown, Methodist. p 128

25 May 1789. Joseph WILLIAMS and Frances Daley, widow. Sur. George Malone. Married by the Rev. John King, Baptist. p 54

27 April 1789. Lewelling WILLIAMS and Elizabeth Hagood. Sur. Gresham Hagood. Married by the Rev. John King, Baptist. p 54

28 April 1781. Miles WILLIAMS and Priscilla Hill, dau. William Hill. Sur. John Williams. p 26

9 March 1804. Robert WILLIAMS and Tempy Wesson. Sur. Sterling Wesson. p 146

12 March 1785. Roger WILLIAMS and Catey Quarles, dau. James Quarles. Sur. John Read. p 35

28 January 1793. Roland WILLIAMS and Nancy Hobby Mares. Sur. John Cheely. Wit. Henry Morris, Sr. Brunswick says Nancy Holiby. Married 31 January by the Rev. Aaron Brown, Methodist, who says Mancy Mares. p 74

July 1788 - July 1789. Thomas WILLIAMS and Mary Jordan. Married by
the Rev. Thomas Lundie, Rector of St. Andrew's Parish. Ministers'
Returns p 354

24 November 1806. Thomas WILLIAMS and Frances Lanier. Sur. John
Williams. p 158

8 May 1798. Wilson WILLIAMS and Sally Allen. Sur. Robert Allen. p 105

29 November 1790. Zebulon WILLIAMS and Nancy Anderton. Sur. Mordecai
Howard. Wit. Edward Berchette, Binns Jones, Bartley Sadler and
Richard Howard. Married by the Rev. Aaron Brown, Methodist. p 61

26 January 1795. Charles WILLIAMSON and Polly Woolsey. Sur. Randolph
Woolsey. Married 28 January by the Rev. Edward Dromgoole. p 84

21 October 1758. Jesse WILLIAMSON and Mary Persons, of age, dau. Thomas
Persons. Sur. Thomas Persons, Jr. Wit. John Persons. p 5

27 March 1805. John R. WILLIAMSON and Betsy Ray. Sur. Green Hill.
p 150

14 April 1790. Joseph WILLIAMSON and Mason Allen (Alley). Consent of
Miles Alley. Sur. John Williamson. Wit. John Fletcher and Harbard
Alley. Married 17 April by the Rev. Edward Dromgoole. p 59

12 July 1778. Lewelling WILLIAMSON and Elizabeth Clack. p 19

28 April 1772. Stephen WILLIAMSON and Anne Collier. Sur. John
Edmondson. Wit. Francis Collier and Lawrence Gibbons, Jr. p 11

- September 1785. Thomas WILLIAMSON and Martha Graves of Albermarle
Parish. Married by the Rev. Thomas Lundie, Rector of St. Andrew's
Parish. Ministers' Returns p 345

17 December 1781. Robert WILLSON and Clara Fisher, dau. James Fisher.
See Robert Wilson. Brunswick p 200

8 December 1797. Benjamin WILSON and Ann Lenoir (Lanier), 21, dau.
Winifred Lenoir (Lanier). Sur. Peter Wynne. Wit. William Latimer.
Married 12 December by the Rev. Peter Wynne. p 101

15 January 1801. John WILSON and Ruth Ramsey. Sur. Peter Traylor. Wit.
Jesse Meachum. Married 16 January by the Rev. Peter Wunne. p 125

17 December 1781. Robert WILSON and Clara Fisher, dau. James Fisher.
Sur. John Wilson. Wit. John Fisher. See Robert Willson. p 27

7 October 1801. Kinchen WINDHAM and Elizabeth Barnes, dau. Stephen
Barnes. Sur. John Wyche. Wit. William Banks. Married by the
Rev. Ira Ellis. p 128

- January 1786. Edward WINFIELD and Frances Smith. Married by the
Rev. Thomas Lundie, Rector of St. Andrew's Parish. Ministers'
Returns p 347

4 November 1777. Joshua WINFIELD and Rebecca Carloss, widow. Sur. Hezekiah Thrower. p 18

22 February 1773. James WITHERS and Judith Brown, widow. Sur. John Powell. p 13

24 December 1787. George WOODLEIF and Katharine Clayton. Sur. Thomas Claiborne. Married by the Rev. John King, Baptist. p 48

22 December 1779. Nathaniel WOODROOF and Caty Vick, dau. John Vick. Sur. Howell Vick. p 23

28 March 1808. George B. WOODRUFF and Salley Manning. Sur. John Wyche. Wit. John Phipps. Married 30 March by the Rev. William Dossey, Baptist. p 166

28 October 1799. Peter WOODSON and Betsey Hobbs, dau. Howell Hobbs. Sur. Benjamin Lashley. Married 14 November by the Rev. Edward Dromgoole. p 115

27 July 1801. Edmund WOODWARD and Jenny Spilman, of age. Sur. John Phipps. p 128

22 October 1804. Edmund WOODWARD and Rebecca Jordan. Sur. John Wilson. p 147

15 November 1803. Orran WOODWARD and Keziah Wallace, 21. Sur. Thomas Connelly. Married 19 November by the Rev. Hubbard Saunders. p 143

15 November 1803. Owen WOODWARD and Keziah Wallace. This is an error; it is Orran Woodward on the original bond. See Orran Woodward. Brunswick p 202

23 November 1795. Abner WOOLSEY and Mary Phipps. Sur. Joseph Phipps. Married 3 December by the Rev. Edward Dromgoole. p 88

23 November 1801. John M. WOOLSEY and Nancy P. Smith. This original bond is for Moore Woolsey. See Moore Woolsey. Brunswick p 202

23 November 1801. Moore WOOLSEY and Nancy P. Smith. Sur. John Smith. Married 25 November by the Rev. Edward Dromgoole. p 129

5 July 1774. Lewelling WORSHAM and Elizabeth Pettway. Sur. Edward Pettway. p 15

24 February 1783. Thomas WORSHAM and Betty Wynne. Sur. John Read. p 30

30 December 1797. Samuel WORTHINGTON and Martha (Patsey) Greenhill. Sur. William Stainback. Wit. Harvey Stainback. Married by the Rev. Aaron Brown, Methodist. p 102

29 April 1789. Braxton WRAY and Mourning Jarrott, 21. Sur. John Wray. Wit. Jeremiah Mize, John Mize, Thomas Saunders and Gray Harwell. Married by the Rev. John King, Baptist. p 54

19 December 1804. Claxton WRAY (or Ray) and Sally Rhea (or Ray). Sur. Eldridge Ray. See Claxton Ray. p 148

6 November 1805. Francis WRAY and Viney Lynch. Married by the Rev. Edward Dromgoole. See Francis Ray. Ministers' Returns p 384

2 January 1801. John WRAY and Patsey Brewer, dau. Greames (?) Brewer. Sur. Claiborne Lightfoot. Wit. John Lightfoot. Married by the Rev. Edward Dromgoole. p 125

27 July 1792. Turner WRAY and Nancy Wesson (or Wray?), dau. Henry Wesson who is surety. p 71

- October 1787. Henry WREN and Sarah Harrison. Married by the Rev. Thomas Lundie, Rector of St. Andrew's Parish. Ministers' Returns p 351

28 November 1791. Jarrot WRIGHT and Tabitha Howell. Sur. James Randall. Wit. John Wright. Married 1 December by the Rev. Edward Dromgoole. p 66

12 October 1796. John WRIGHT and Polly Brewer. Sur. Willis Brewer. Wit. Reuben Wright. Married 13 October by the Rev. Edward Dromgoole. p 92

28 November 1808. Josias WRIGHT and Sally Wright. Sur. Wesley Wright. Returned 29 December by the Rev. Edward Dromgoole. p 168

17 January 1809. Merritt WRIGHT and Nancy Owens. Sur. Samuel Wright. Married 18 January by the Rev. Edward Dromgoole. p 170

3 January 1795. Samuel WRIGHT and Sally Owens, 21. George Wright and Sophia Wright make affidavit as to her age. Sur. George Wright. Wit. Mary Manning. Married 15 January by the Rev. Edward Dromgoole. p 84

July 1788 - July 1789. Sterling WRIGHT and Silvey Davis. Married by the Rev. John King, Baptist. Ministers' Returns p 354

3 October 1804. Sterling WRIGHT and Sally Hill. Married by the Rev. Aaron Brown, Methodist. Ministers' Returns p 386

27 November 1809. Wesley WRIGHT and Creecy Birdsong. Sur. Henry Birdson. p 173

20 December 1810. Wesley WRIGHT and Mary M. Person. Sur. Drury Person. Married by the Rev. Cary James, Methodist. p 178

29 January 1755. James WYCHE and Leah Maclin. Sur. Nicholas Edmunds. James Wyche of Albermarle Parish, Sussex County. Leah Maclin of St. Andrew's Parish, Brunswick County. Wit. Lett. Tazwell. p 2

3 September 1802. John WYCHE and Polley Hobbs, born 17 February 1782, dau. Hubbard and Martha (Meredith) Hobbs. Sur. George Atkins. Wit. John Hobbs. Married 14 September by the Rev. Ira Ellis. p 135

24 January 1790. Nathaniel WYCHE and Middleton Fletcher. Sur. James Fletcher. Wit. John Fletcher and O.M. Fletcher. Married 3 February by the Rev. Edward Dromgoole. p 58

14 September 1782. Peter WYCHE and Patty Harrison, dau. Benjamin Harrison. Sur. Charles Harrison. Wit. Lewis Brewer and William Walker. Peter Wyche under age, son of Henry Wyche. p 29

13 January 1783. Gillanus WYNN and Rebecca Lester, 21, dau. Andrew Lester, and sister of Francis Lester who is surety. Gillanus Wynn of Lundenburg County. p 30

23 November 1772. John WYNN and Mary Lyell or Lyall. Sur. Joseph Lyall. Wit. Ann Lyell. p 12

20 January 1802. Lewallen WYNNE and Elizabeth Freeman. Sur. Hamlin Freeman. Married 21 January by the Rev. Hubbard Saunders. p 132

16 February 1802. John WYNNE and Citiviah Malone, 21. Sur. Jordan Malone. Married 17 February by the Rev. Peter Wynne. p 133

25 October 1790. John WYNNE and Mary Ingram, of age. Sur. Jesse Penn. Wit. Robert Latimer. Married by the Rev. Thomas Lundie, Rector of St. Andrew's Parish who says Elizabeth Ingram. p 61

27 September 1808. John WYNNE and Charlotte Edwards. Sur. Esau Goodwyn. p 168

8 December 1797. Peter WYNNE, Jr. and Winifred Wilson, dau. John Wilson. Sur. Benjamin Wilson. Wit. William Latimer. Married 13 December by the Rev. Peter Wynne. p 101

9 August 1753. Robert WYNNE and Mary Philipson. Sur. Lawrence Gibbons. Robert Wynne of Surry County. p 1

16 March 1808. William WYNNE and Polly Wynne. Sur. Peter Wynne. Married 17 March by the Rev. Peter Wynne. p 166

13 March 1810. Benjamin P. YATES and Elizabeth F. Stith, dau. G. Stith. Sur. William Yates. Wit. David B. Stith. p 175

- September 1785. William YATES and Elizabeth Booth of Albermarle Parish. Married by the Rev. Thomas Lundie, Rector of St. Andrew's Parish. Ministers' Returns p 345

14 February 1792. William YEARGAN and Elizabeth Rainey, 21. Howell Duggar makes affidavit as to her age. Sur. Thomas Jones. Wit. Daniel Dugger and Richmond Dugger. Married 16 February by the Rev. Aaron Brown, Methodist. p 69

7 January 1785. Thomas YEARGIN and Patty Burrow. Sur. Miles House. p 35

23 January 1805. Charles YOUNG and Mary Harwell. Married by the Rev. Peter Wynne. Ministers' Returns p 382

25 January 1796. William YEARGIN and Rebecca Bennett. Sur. John Bennett. Married by the Rev. Aaron Brown, Methodist. p 90

- -   1789. Coleman YOUNG and Mary Standley. Married by the
Rev. John King, Baptist. Ministers' Returns p 354

24 September 1794. Samuel YOUNG, Jr., and Elizabeth Love, dau. Fanny
Love, ward of John Drummond. Sur. Willie Harrison. Married
25 September by the Rev. Edward Dromgoole. p 82

19 December 1791. Cornelius ZACHARY and Jenny Haymour. Brunswick p 205

DUGGAR - DUGGER,
  Armon 25
  Elizabeth 90
  Fanny 12, 80
  Frances 79
  Luvaney 77
  Nancy 66
  Polly 57
  Sally 26, 60
  Sarah 80
DUNKLEY,
  Elizabeth 94
  Martha 55
DUNN,
  Frances 85
  Nancy 44
DUNNINGTON,
  Elizabeth 47
DUPREE,
  Eliza Donaldson 95
DURHAM,
  Clarissa 3

EASTER,
  Mary 2
EAVES,
  Amey 35
  Elizabeth 81
EDMONDSON,
  Sarah 84
EDMUNDS,
  Ann 102
  Charlotte 59
  Clarissa 80
  Elizabeth 33, 57
  Julia 60
  Mary 58
  Middy 18
  Polly 77
  Rahab 51
  Sally 30
  Sarah 85
  Susan 52
EDWARDS,
  Brambley 53
  Charity 77
  Charlotte 110
  Diannah 105
  Dolly 66
  Elizabeth 66
  Martha 48
  Mary 2, 3, 7, 82
  Nancy (3) 26
  Obedience 77
  Patsey 98
  Permely 79
  Rebecca 18
  Sarah 65
  Susanna 70
  Tabitha 98
  Temperance 4, 42
ELDER,
  Blanche 1
  Nancy 7, 11
  Phebe 22
  Rebecca 56
  Susanna J. 53
ELDRIDGE,
  Sarah 27
ELLICE,
  Nancy 43
ELLIOTT,
  Mary 99
  Nancy Willis 9
  Sarah 99
ELMORE,
  Polly 77
EMBREY - EMBRY,
  Martha 87
  Priscilla 44
EMMERY,
  Tempe 99

EPPES - EPPS,
  Susanna 106
  Tabitha 101
EVANS,
  Elizabeth 106
  Susanna 34, 50
EVES,
  Tabitha 54
EZELL,
  Dolly W. 85
  Sally 90
  Susanna 15, 30

F -,
  Frances 8
FANN,
  Lucretia 96
FIELD,
  Henrietta M. 67
  Margaret B. 62
FINCH,
  Polly 32
  Rebecca 7
FIRTH,
  Elizabeth 80
  Polly 13
  Polly B. 25
  Sally 79
  Sarah 79
  Rebecca 1
FISHER,
  Anne 88
  Clara (2) 107
  Constance 78
  Martha 29
  Polly 38
  Sarah 23
FLAX,
  Nancy 53
FLETCHER,
  Middleton 109
  Nancy A. 65
  Rebecca 56
  Rebecca J. 6
  Sally 6
FLOOD,
  Mary 70
FLOYD,
  Amy 66
  Ann 73
  Elizabeth 62
  Martha 66
  Nancy 102
  Sally 31
FORT,
  Elizabeth 82
  Lucy 88
  Marian 42
  Martha 88
  Sally (2) 20
FOSTER,
  Dolly 35
  Elizabeth H. 106
  Susanna 65
FOWLKES,
  Elizabeth 73
  Lucy 97
  Polly Ginnings 37
FOX,
  Winifred 83
FREEMAN,
  Agnes 100
  Elizabeth 77, 110
  Lucy 104
FUNN,
  Lucretia 96

GARGUS,
  Nancy 88
GARRETT,
  Susanna 98
GARRISS,
  Lydia, 59

GARY,
  Nancy 39
GEE,
  Betsey 46
  Bridgett 24
  Elizabeth 40
  Hannah 76
  Mary 20
  Nancy 19
  Parthenia 71
  Penelope 76
  Priscilla 23
  Sally 102
  Susanna 82
GEORGE,
  Lucy 87
GHOLSON,
  Elizabeth 32
  Martha 41
  Nancy 76
  Patsy 41
GIBS,
  Delitha 92
GILLIAM,
  Ann 9
  Celia 19
  Elizabeth 71
  Selah 19
GINNINGS,
  Frances M. 1
GLANDISH,
  Betsey (2) 40
  Martha 10
GOODRICH,
  Elizabeth B. 34
  Molly 11
  Nancy Kemp 39
  Polly 39
  Sally 10
  Sarah 95
GOODRUM,
  Polly 49
GRANGER,
  Polly 53
GRANT,
  Dolly 56
GRAVES,
  Martha 107
GREGORY,
  Oney 68
GREEN,
  Ann 81
  Elizabeth 60
  Lucy 34
  Patty 47
  Polly 6
  Sally J. 38
GREENHILL,
  Catherine C. 49
  Martha 108
  Patsy 108
GRESHAM,
  Christianna 101
  Mary 46
GRIGG,
  Patty 9
GRIFFIES,
  Sally 15
GRIFFITH,
  Nancy 68
GRUBBS,
  Elizabeth 72, 76, 78
  Susanna 80
GUNN,
  Nancy 66
  Susanna 104

HAGOOD,
  Elizabeth 6, 106
HAILEY - HALEY,
  Caty 36
  Dolly 81

HALL,
  Lucy 44, (2) 101
  Martha 16
  Rebecca 3
  Sarah 21
HAMILTON,
  Susanna 59
HAMLETT,
  Writter 63
HAMMON - HAMMOND,
  Betsey L. 49
  Nancy 5
  Patsey 31
HAMOUR,
  Tabitha 37
HAMPTON,
  Elizabeth 69
  Jean 44
  Nancy 65
HANCOCK - HANCOCKE,
  Anthania 40
  Dorothy 40
  Elizabeth 28
  Patsey 48
  Polly 61
HARDAWAY,
  Anne 17
  Elizabeth 99
  Frances (2) 16
  Mary 17
  Mason 12
  Nancy 73
  Rebecca 2, 67
  Sarah 90
HARDIE - HARDY,
  Ann 18
  Elizabeth 62
HARPER,
  Judith 97
  Lucy 2
  Rebecca 73
  Sally 35
HARRIS,
  Patty 5
  Priscilla 65
  Sarah 18
  Susanna 91
HARRISON,
  Ann 99
  Anne 42, 43
  Christian 39
  Elizabeth 31, 40
  Frances 58, 71
  Frances T. 87
  Jane 82
  Lucy 58
  Martha 9, 11, 56
  Mary 76
  Nancy 22, 55, 101
  Naomy 56
  Olive 63, 89
  Patty 110
  Polly 76, 91
  Sarah 109
  Sarah Ann 54
  Silvia 11
  Tabitha 9, 19, 21
HARTWELL,
  Betsey 33
  Nancy 89
  Polley 45
HARWELL,
  Amy 74
  Ann 59
  Elizabeth 12
  Frances 54
  Mary 110
  Nancy 80
  Patsey 35
  Sarah 61, 82
  Susanna 1, 93
HASKINS,
  Martha (2) 27

HASKINS, (Continued)
  Sarah S. 14
HAWKS,
  Martha 23
HAWTHORN,
  Rebecca 64
HAYMOUR,
  Jane 93
  Jenny 111
HEARN,
  Elizabeth 24
  Jane 25
  Martha 65
  Mary 104
HICKS,
  Elizabeth 15, 38
  Elizabeth B. 9
  Frances 37, 102
  Hannah 17
  Jean 73
  Judith 19
  Nancy V. 100
  Polly 40
  Rebecca 9
  Sally 9, 42
  Sarah 38
  Susanna Elizabeth 101
  Tabitha 10, 34
HICKMAN,
  Lucy 67
HIGH,
  Sally 95
HIGHT,
  Sarah 21
HIGHTOWER,
  Hannah 98
  Martha 26
  Mary B. 96
  Sarah 19
HILL,
  Hannah 71
  Nancy 30
  Priscilla 106
  Sally 109
  Sarah 96
  Temperance 18
HIX,
  Mary 4
HOBBS,
  Betsey 30, 108
  Lucy 45
  Polley 109
  Sally 60
HOGWOOD,
  Sally 89
HOLDERBY,
  Mary C. 94, 96
HOLLOWAY,
  Betsy 38
  Jamima 72
  Martha 38
  Nelly 41
  Quentena 50
  Timna 10
HOOD,
  Polley 6
  Sarah 50
HOUSE - HOWSE,
  Catharine 79
  Frances (2) 86
  Martha 100
  Milly 68
  Nancy 102
  Tabitha 106
  Winifred 9
HOWARD,
  Elizabeth 68
  Hannah (2) 103
HOWELL,
  Tabitha 109
HOWERTON,
  Elizabeth 23
  Sally 77

HOY,
  Elizabeth 50
HUBBARD,
  Lucy 57
HUDGINS,
  Mary Callis 43
HUDSON,
  Phebe 84
HUFF,
  Elizabeth (2) 90
  Milly 10
  Molly Monk 11
  Olive 67
  Tabitha 46
HULMAN,
  Sally 25
HULUISE,
  Sally 25
HUNNICUTT,
  Caroline 88
  Mary L. 91
  Sally P. 47
  Susan 54
HUNT,
  Ann 36, 37
  Clary 4
  Sarah 14
HUNTER,
  Elizabeth 33
HUSKEY,
  Amy 80
  Oney 80
HUTCHINS,
  Martha 30
HYDE,
  Letitia 36

INGRAM,
  Ann 7
  Charlotte 73
  Elizabeth 27, 103, 110
  Eliza G. 104
  Eliza H. 5
  Gracy 100
  Mary 110
  Mary Ann 47, 97
  Nancy 38
  Patty 18
  Polly 24
  Sally 28
  Sarah 24
  Susan 13
  Susanna 37, 45
IRBY,
  Elizabeth 92
IVEY - IVIE - IVY,
  Nancy Harrison 30
  Patty 41
  Rebecca 34

JACKSON,
  - 55
  Anna 67
  Eliza 80
  Fortune 63
  Hannah 4
  Mary 96
  Nancy 35
  Patsy 20
  Patty 20
  Polly 8, 13, 105
  Rebecca Ann 12
  Sally 24
  Sarah 4, 20
  Susanna 49
JAMES,
  Charlotte 91
  Elizabeth 10
  Frances L. 3
  Martha 37
  Polly 100
  Sally 32

MARKS,
  Nancy 69
  Polly B. 28
  Rebecca 12
MASON,
  Frances 6
  Jincy 102
  Mary W. 63
  Polly 48
  Rebecca 59
  Sally 47
MASSEY,
  Delilah 103
MATHEWS - MATTHEWS,
  Betsey 50
  Hannah 44
  Jean 93
  Jincy 93
  Lucy 7
  Mary 71, 91
  Nancy 28
MATHIS - MATTHIS,
  Angelica Jones 62
  Anglica 100
  Anna 38
  Betsey 89
  Mary 71
  Sarah 29
MAYS,
  Elizabeth 5
MC CAN,
  Martha 81
MC KENNEY - MC KENNY,
  Delilah 98
  Dicey 98
  Elizabeth 54
  Sally 22
  Susanna (2) 3
MEADE,
  Ann 30
  Mariah 91
  Susanna 31
MEANLEY,
  Martha 63
  Mary 63
MEREDITH,
  Anne 98
  Elizabeth 83
  Mary W. 7
  Salley 70
MERRIOTT,
  Mary 29
MERRITT,
  Eliza 83
MILLER,
  Mary 11
  Nancy 50
  Susanna 12
MISKELL,
  Frances 62, 65
  Rebecca 36
  Winifred Beckwith 33
MITCHELL,
  Ann 14
  Betty 38
  Jane 4
  Mary 11
  Rebecca 4
  Scotty 14
MIZE - MIZES,
  Judy 48
  Lucretia 100
  Martha 64
  Mary 100
  Sarah 95
  Tabitha 8
MOODY,
  Patsey 64
MOORE,
  Ann 64
  Betsey 53
  Elizabeth 53, 93
  Fanny 56

MOORE, (Continued)
  Frances 89
  Martha 3
  Milly 93
  Nancy 100
  Sally 30
MORRIS,
  Elizabeth 96
  Martha L. 61
  Patsey 17
  Rebecca 62
  Sarah 14, 69
MOSELEY,
  Abby 44
  Amey 57
  Hulda 46
  Mansfield 8
  Nelly 66
  Noah 95
  Patsey 94, 95
  Rebecca 46
  Rody 89
  Sally 57
  Sarah 18
  Tabitha 67
  Thirza - Thirzor 56
MOSS,
  Betsey 52
  Sally 44
MURRELL,
  Elizabeth 17
  Nancy 74
MYRICK,
  Sarah 102

NANNY,
  Amey 82
  Charlotte 105
  Elizabeth 27
  Jinsey 30
  Middy 104
  Molley 104
  Oney 82
  Rebecca 102
  Rhoda 65
  Ritter 89
  Sally 102
  Winifred 10
NASH,
  Elizabeth 45
  Rebecca 21
NEAL,
  Elizabeth 45
  Joanna D. 88
  Mary 15
  Nancy 85
NICHOLSON,
  Elizabeth 11
NIPPER,
  Ann 31
  Nancy 5
NOLLY,
  Elizabeth 83
NORRIS,
  Atlheliah 46
NORTH,
  Sally 31

OAST,
  Sarah 54
OGBORNE - OGBURN,
  Eliza 93
  Martha 93
  Mary 93
  Tabitha 51
OLDHAM,
  Ann 42
ORGAIN,
  Lucy 1
  Sally 74
OVERBY,
  Angline 52
  Elizabeth 47

OVERBY, (Continued)
  Keziah 64
  Nancy 94
  Patty (2) 75
OWEN - OWENS,
  Eleanor Hughs 29
  Lovey 88
  Martha 55
  Mary 60
  Nancy 42, 109
  Sally 109

PARHAM,
  Elizabeth 64
  Frances 35, 45
  Mary Branch 55
  Nancy 13
  Obedience Turpin 53
  Rebecca 34
  Sally Prudence 9
  Sarah 4
  Susan 56, 78
  Tabitha 41
PARISH,
  Elizabeth 2
  Jane 22
  Sarah 76
PARKER,
  Elizabeth 54
  Rebecca 106
  Temperance 28
PAUP,
  Priscilla 10
PAYNE,
  Elizabeth (2) 101
PEACE,
  Elizabeth 65
  Lucy 65
PEARSON,
  Cesley 103
  Patsey 11
  Rebecca 102
PEEBLES,
  Mary 55
  Susanna 95
PEGRAM,
  Susanna 3
PENN,
  Catherine 68
  Nancy S. 52
  Sally 38
PENNINGTON,
  Betsy 74
  Fatha 67
  Lucy 33
  Mary (2) 30
  Sally 52
PENTICOST,
  Peggy 84
PEPPER,
  Elizabeth 54
PERSON - PERSONS,
  Mary 107
  Mary M. 109
PERRY,
  Jeanny 33
  Lucy 69
  Polly C. 94
  Priscilla 89
PETERSON,
  Frances 76
  Temperance 93
PETILLO - PITELLO,
  Mildred 54
  Rebecca 6
  Sally 58
PETTIT,
  Lucy 43
PETTWAY,
  Cicily 60
  Elizabeth 108
  Lucy 7

PHILIPSON,
  Mary 110
PHILLIPS,
  Patty 52
  Polly 28
  Prudence 64
  Susanna 86
PHIPPS,
  Mary 108
PHOENIX,
  Elizabeth 75
PIERCY,
  Elizabeth 78
PILKINGTON,
  Betsy 15, 52
PITMAN,
  Susanna 59
POOL,
  Mary 65
PORCH,
  Elizabeth 101
  Susan 48
PORTER,
  Lucy 25
  Nancy 10
  Polly 79
POTTS,
  Elizabeth 73
  Nancy 16
  Patsey 37
POWELL,
  Elizabeth 14, 99
  Jean 43
  Jincy P. (2) 48
  Lucy 8
  Mary 90
  Nancy 68
  Polly 76
  Rebecca 38
  Sally 76, 95
PRESTON,
  Martha 7
PRICE,
  Elizabeth (2) 26
  Sylvia 38
PRITCHETT,
  Elizabeth 3
  Lucy 97
  Polly 29
  Susanna 33
PROCTOR,
  Suckey 77
PURKINSON,
  Elizabeth 11

QUARLES,
  Catey 106
  Mary 12, 97
  Nancy 62, 80
  Polly S. 97
  Sally Ball 95
  Susanna 10

RAGLAND,
  Macarina 3
RAGSDALE,
  Nancy 32
RAMSEY,
  Ruth 107
RAINES,
  Elizabeth N. G. 37
  Lucy 87
RAINEY - RANEY,
  Elizabeth 28, 110
  Mary 26
  Selah 96
RANDOLPH,
  Lucy 49
RATTENBURG,
  Lucy 22
RAWLINGS,
  Dolly 37
  Nancy 94

RAWLINGS, (Continued)
  Polly 72
  Sally 31
  Vicey 71
RAY,
  Amey 64
  Betsy 107
  Sally 80, 109
READ,
  Nancy 1
  Pharaby 46
  Polly 28
  Silvey 36
READE,
  Jean 5
REDDING,
  Rebecca (2) 32
REESE,
  Betsy 75
  Mary 85
  Rebecca 54
  Susanna 11
RHEA,
  Cinthia 45
  Ritter 15
  Sally 109
RICE,
  Peggy 99
RICHARDSON,
  Frances 48
  Lucy 35
  Mary 83
  Sarah 70
RIDEOUT,
  Dolly 67
  Jane 16
  Lucy 99
RIEVES - RIVES,
  Betty 83
  Tabitha 70
RIVERS,
  Anne 20
  Elizabeth 6, 82
  Hannah 65
  Martha 11
ROBERSON - ROBERTSON,
  Mary 16, 73
  Rebecca 83
ROBERTS,
  Ann H. 68
  Rebecca 103
ROBINSON,
  Fanny 21
  Polly 104
  Sally 83
ROGERS,
  Delphia 87
  Elizabeth 61
  Rebecca 69
ROLLINS,
  Lucy 36
ROPER,
  Mary M. 39
ROSE,
  Eleanor 97
  Lucy 86
  Mary 84
  Rebecca 92
ROSS,
  Amey 96
  Liddia 36
ROSSER,
  Bathin - Bethea 81
RUSSELL,
  Ann 71
  Caty 53
RYLAND,
  Salley 96

SADLER,
  Anney 1
  Mary 69

SAMFORD,
  Elizabeth 26, 85
  Hannah 49
  Jeany 53
  Jincey 53
  Mary 33
SAMMONS,
  Dicey 92
  Fanny 92
  Vicey 92
SAUNDERS,
  Betsy 27
  Celeys 55
  Elizabeth 25
  Jincey 15
  Lucy 74
  Margaret 94
  Martha 85
  Mary 33
  Nancy 6
  Sally 74, 85
  Selah 55
  Sinah (2) 14
SCARBROUGH,
  Anne 78
  Lucy 57
  Rebecca 97
  Sally 47
SCOTT,
  Lucy 77
SEAWELL,
  Elizabeth 59
  Mary 44
SEWARD,
  Caty 64
  Elizabeth 61
  Fanny 69
  Margaret 101
  Martha 68
  Patsey 28
  Polly 63
  Rebecca 13
  Sabra 103
  Sally 60
  Tabitha 103
SERIVANT,
  Lucy 60
SEXTON,
  Mary 37
SHELBURNE,
  Mary 58
SHELL,
  Betsey 7
  Leodicia 94
SHELTON,
  Betty 84
SHEPPERSON,
  Mary 28
SHIP,
  Sally 35
SHORT,
  Elizabeth 78
  Fanny (2) 17
  Mabel 86
  Martha 53
  Nancy 26
  Patty 53
  Rebecca 86
  Sally 40, 45
  Susanna 53
SILLS,
  Sally 17
SIMMONS,
  Ermine 27
  Jane 12
  Lucy 50
  Martha 30, 54
  Mary 50, 96
  Mason 66
SIMMS - SIMS,
  Elizabeth 4, 45, 105
  Mary 3

www.ingramcontent.com/pod-product-compliance
Lightning Source LLC
Chambersburg PA
CBHW021834020426
42334CB00014B/619